A Jacana book

Mail & Guardian
Bedside Book
2003

edited by
Shaun de Waal

This selection © *Mail & Guardian* & Jacana 2003

ISBN 1-919931-83-X

Published by Jacana
5 St Peter Rd
Bellevue
2198
South Africa

Cover design by Disturbance
john@disturbance.co.za

Internal design by Indent

Printed by Formeset Printers, Cape Town

See a complete list of Jacana titles at **www.jacana.co.za**

Contents

Mondli Makhanya Foreword **7**
Elisabeth Lickindorf Our grasping ancestry **9**
Gavin Evans 'Extinct' San reap rewards **12**
Fiona Macleod Jumbo poo is good for you **16**
LETTER: Simple science **18**
David Macfarlane True lies or false truths? **19**
Jaspreet Kindra Neither saint nor saviour **21**
Athelé Wills A world gone crazy **25**
LETTERS: American nightmare / There's no place like home / The grass *is* greener on the other side **30**
Jeff Guy Lessons from imperial history **32**
Mondli Makhanya A war of whores **36**
LETTERS: A reckless, criminal disregard for life / Don't whine about the bully / Show us, Helen **38**
Tom Eaton Wanted: Comical Ali **41**
John Matshikiza Spooked by colour-coding **43**
LETTER: in brief **46**
Drew Forrest Mbeki goes for the jugular **46**
Itumeleng Mahabane For whom has the tide turned? **48**
Fikile-Ntsikelelo Moya Case bares SA's racial bones **52**
John Matshikiza Still no Happy ending **55**
Rapule Tabane Just another dorpie **57**
Robert Kirby Another Dullah Omar brainchild pregnancy goes pop **61**
Marianne Merten Looking for an MP in a haystack **63**
Mondli Makhanya In search of a new moral DNA **66**
LETTERS: ANC's conscience lies in the gutter / ANC is milking the country dry **68**
Stefaans Brümmer and Sam Sole Oil scandal rocks SA **69**
Stefaans Brümmer and Sam Sole Hey, what's going on here? **78**
Stefaans Brümmer It all started here **82**
Editorial Madiba, we thank you **84**
LETTERS: Madiba, a true world leader **85**
LETTER: in brief **86**
Editorial We must not fear to dream **87**

LETTER: Once were warriors **88**
Zackie Achmat The long walk to civil disobedience **90**
Nawaal Deane The madness of Queen Manto **93**
Edwin Cameron The dead hand of denialism **96**
Nawaal Deane A fight for life over death **103**
Ferial Haffajee African growth slows **105**
Wisani wa ka Ngobeni 'We have no food, no work and no money' **108**
LETTER: Drought of good governance **116**
Sean O'Toole The unstoppable tide **117**
Justin Pearce One year after Savimbi **120**
Shaun de Waal Tears of rage **125**
LETTER: in brief **127**
Matthew Krouse Home is where the hurt is **128**
Tebogo Alexander Hail King Louis! **131**
Editorial Pity he's Australian now **135**
François Ebersöhn Art battles at the mall **136**
Zebulon Dread In awe of balls and batterers **138**
LETTERS: Relax, Mr Dread / Peace is more important than play **143**
Gavin Foster Fighting for the Lord **144**
Julia Beffon Mills & Boon meets the gynae **147**
Bismarck Masangu A little wet dream problem **149**
Xolisa Vitsha Gay dreams bruise straight egos **151**
Yolandi Groenewald My big fat Afrikaner wedding **153**
LETTERS: Big fat Afrikaner wedding memories **155**
Marianne Merten Sea Point 'unrecognisable' as gangs move in **156**
Pat Sidley and news reporters SA's Lord Haw Haw was dedicated 'news junkie' **158**
LETTERS: Johnson was no Lord Haw Haw **160**
Editorial How to honour this titan? **161**
LETTER: Sisulu's monument **163**
(David Beresford) Dear Walter **164**
LETTER: Best wishes from Walter **166**
Fikile-Ntsikelelo Moya Eish, farewell Slow Poison **166**
Brian McDonald 'He's an old dog that can't bite' **168**
Paul Fauvet Cardoso's last, greatest report **170**
John Matshikiza From altar boy to revolutionary **173**

Foreword

Mondli Makhanya
Editor, Mail & Guardian

George W Bush took the world to war — and to hell — in 2003. Walter Sisulu died and went to heaven this year. Eighteen-year-old Abbey Mzayiya found his real identity and the first signs of happiness. Then there was Jacob Zuma versus Bulelani Ngcuka. Our contributor Bismarck Masangu found himself having gay wet dreams and was told (by another contributor) that it was okay. The irrepressible Zebulon Dread (helped by a forthright poster) immortalised the phrase "Blah, blah, fucken blah!" and got the *Mail & Guardian* into trouble with the Mother Grundies. HIV/Aids continued to eat into our economic and social fabric.

That, in part, was 2003 through the eyes of the *Mail & Guardian*, the African continent's most authoritiave and best-written newspaper.

As journalists we have a ringside seats at the dramas unfolding around us — and are able to lead society in its thinking, crying, laughing and dancing. The *Mail & Guardian* certainly tried to achieve that feat this year, and we hope we did not disappoint. Our large community of writers, commentators and letter contributors had their collective fingers on the world's pulse — reflecting and responding intelligently to the unfolding dramas around them.

If future historians one day ask what defined 2003, the nation will probably be divided between the global events — the war in Iraq — and domestic issues such as the war between Ngcuka and Zuma. Both these strands, and more, are catered for in this book, which takes the reader a whirlwhind tour of 2003.

On returning from a holiday in the United States, freelance writer Athelé Wills questioned the eating and spending habits of Americans — "a once-great nation of people ... brainwashed into becoming a compliant herd of sheeplike voracious consumers". This view took on a broader significance when such worship of ignorance and consumerism gave George W Bush licence to hoodwink Americans into going to war against Iraq.

This war is an issue on which *Mail & Guardian* writers waxed lyrical — and contentious — from Jeff Guy's drawing parallels between Britain's 1879 rabble-rousing on the eve of the invasion of the Zulu kingdom to our coinage, "War of the whores".

On the pages that follow are stories of pain, anger and exhilaration at the South African government's confusing response to HIV/Aids. This virus and its associated syndrome of diseases has brought much suffering to millions of South Africans. But it has also produced heroes out of those who have defied the virus. These angry, heroic voices resonate through the pages of this *Bedside Book*. Zackie Achmat explains the position of his organisation, the Treatment Action Campaign, in its return to civil disobedience — and his one-on-one spat with the Minister of Health (some of whose eccentricities we detailed in a now-famous piece, "The madness of Queen Manto", also included in this volume). In "The dead hand of denialism", Judge Edwin Cameron writes that the government's attitude "continues to bedevil our response to the disease".

Then hear the voice of Nombuyiselo Maphongwane, whose story of bravery plucked at the hearts of an American family who pledged a year's supply of anti-retrovirals to her. After nearly two months of taking the drugs and braving their side-effects, she was able to declare triumphantly: "I am so excited because I can eat a whole tennis biscuit now." Let us hope that in next year's *Mail & Guardian Bedside Book* we will be able to tell more such stories.

South Africans also partied hard in 2003, celebrating Madiba's 85th birthday, hailing the return for a home-soil performance of Blue Notes great Louis Moholo, and marking small but significant steps towards normalcy.

This society, in all its contradictions, is what this *Bedside Book* — the fifth in a popular series — hopes to evoke.

All gratitude to Shaun de Waal, who applied his deep and vast literary mind to the selection of the finest and most memorable writing from Africa's finest newspaper. Thanks also to Drew Forrest for his help in compiling the selection of letters from our readers, and to Sewela Mohale, our librarian, for her consummate filing skills.

Our grasping ancestry

Elisabeth Lickindorf

Dramatic new finds at the Cradle of Humankind at Sterkfontein near Krugersdorp could change well-established ideas about human evolution, says one of the world's most prominent palaeoanthropologists.

Ron Clarke of Wits University, who leads the team that has been laboriously excavating the Little Foot skeleton at the site since 1997, says the fossil indicates that man did not descend from knuckle-walking apes. The most recent finds lead Clarke to draw unexpected conclusions about how our ancestors moved about, how we might have evolved, and critical differences between us and apes such as gorillas, chimpanzees, orang-utans and gibbons.

Clarke, Stephen Motsumi and Nkwane Molefe uncovered the lower legs of the 3,3-million-year-old *Australopithecus* in 1997, the skull in 1998, its left arm and hand in 1999, and more recently the upper part of the right thigh bone, the crushed pelvis, ribs and vertebrae of the lower back. The team estimates it might take another year to expose the rest of the skeleton.

Little Foot is the most complete fossil of its kind anywhere in the world, and the only one ever found where the hands and feet were associated with the same individual's arms and legs. The combined evidence from the skeleton makes Clarke question the common view that humans derive from a forebear that walked on all fours, using its knuckles as a chimpanzee does.

Clarke believes our ancestor is more likely to have walked upright from the start and to have been a slow climber when in the trees. "This is our first-ever hand, the first time we've got a hand with an arm, and the first time ever we've got a complete arm with a complete leg that belong to the same individual," he says. "So for the very first time we can talk about ratios [of one body part to another]. Prior to this, it's all been surmise."

The important thing about Little Foot's hand, he reports, is that the palm is short and the thumb is well developed and long compared with the fingers. "The shape and proportions are the same as those of our modern human hand and different from the apes with their relatively much shorter thumbs, longer palms and longer curved fingers."

Hand shape and proportions, he says, tell us how different animals move about in trees. They can either run along branches, as many small creatures do, they can climb around slowly in a vertical position like a koala bear, or they can hang beneath the branches by their arms. "If you're suspended from the branches it's advantageous to have a long hand with curved fingers that you can use as a hook. But a long thumb gets in the way, especially if, like a gibbon, you move very fast through the trees, swinging beneath the branches with arm-over-arm movements.

"At some time, the ancestors of chimps, gorillas and orangs spent more time suspending themselves from branches and they developed long hands with curved fingers and relatively short thumbs. Their long arms relative to their short legs also didn't evolve for nothing — they're advantageous in that kind of locomotion because the longer the arm the more distance you can cover in a shorter time through the branches."

When these apes moved along the ground, says Clarke, they could either run on the ground as the gibbon does, with arms extended in the air to keep them out of the way, or they could use arms as props, knuckle-walking on all fours and using their hands with the long curved fingers for support. The proportion of arm to leg length of the Little Foot hominid is quite different, says Clarke. Instead of the long arms and short legs characteristic of apes, its arms and legs are about the same length.

Clarke's conclusions are sure to arouse debate. The hand, he contends, tells us that our ancestors were probably never knuckle-walkers and that when they were in the trees they were slow branch-climbers. "They would grasp branches powerfully, with fingers around one side and thumb around the other. They'd have moved the way children move about on a jungle gym today. It's in our genes. We see gymnasts and circus performers climbing by grasping with their hands — they can go straight up a vertical pole, and you'll see them gripping with their feet and their knees as they shimmy up."

We cannot yet say that one or other form of *Australopithecus* was ancestral to modern humans, says Clarke. "But when you look at a fossil you see features that are held over from an ancestry, and you see specialised features that separate out from other creatures and make it part of a new species: it very seldom happens that a specialised feature reverts back to the unspecialised form."

The Little Foot skeleton's hand, argues Clarke, shows how "early, primitive [equally long] digits — such as those of a crocodile, for instance — can evolve in different directions. My contention is that the ancestor of the *Australopithecus* with the human-like hand always had this kind of hand, and retained it. The thumb is useful for climbing and for gripping branches in this pincer-like way.

"Descendants of *Australopithecus* in the form of *Homo* [the human genus] had this sort of hand too, which they found useful for making and using tools. That's why we're so adept — everything we have we owe to our slow-climbing arboreal ancestry.

"My argument is that chimps may not, as has previously been supposed, be our closest relatives after all. If the ancestors of humans were specialised knuckle-walkers like chimps and gorillas, they would have kept the long arms, palm, and fingers as well as the short thumbs that these apes had developed. In contrast with Little Foot's more or less equally proportioned arms and legs, however, modern humans have developed longer legs than arms, because leaving the trees to become fully terrestrial and bipedal made longer legs advantageous for covering greater distances on the ground in a single stride. You can see how the greatest runners have the longest legs."

Still in the ground and, Clarke hopes, waiting to be found are the skeleton's right arm and shoulder-blade, the rest of the spinal column, kneecaps, and perhaps a collarbone, which is rare for early hominids. "But one's got to be patient," he says. "This work can be frustrating and very disheartening. Every time we put in the smallest chisel and we're tempted to work a bit faster, we have to remember that if we go too aggressively we can go through bone before we know it. But at the back of our minds ... we know that the rest has to be there. That's what keeps us going.

"When people ask 'How long until we get it all out?' I have to say, 'It's been in the ground three and a half million years — a year or two is as nothing to it.' The important thing is to find everything, and not to damage it." **31.01**

Ron Clarke's findings are published in the SA Journal of Science

'Extinct' San reap rewards

Gavin Evans

Piet Rooi adjusts his Union Jack cap, pushes his glasses up his nose and smiles at the inanity of my question about why he used the hoodia plant. "*Hoekom* [Why]?" he asks. "Because it helps us survive." He holds up a hand to forestall further interrogation. "I eat the *xhoba* [hoodia] to stave off hunger and thirst and then I no longer feel hungry or thirsty. I eat it when I am feeling weak and then I feel strong and virile. I eat it when I have a bad stomach or flu and then I feel better."

It hasn't rained for almost a year in this remote part of the South African Kalahari, near the South African-Botswana border, but after a 15 minute trot in the 42°C heat, Rooi has no trouble finding the cucumber-shaped cactus plant "We're in drought now, so I'll braai it because it's too bitter to eat raw," this 73-year-old former farmworker explains while picking two branches, "but when it rains it turns brighter green and has a nice, sour taste and I can chew it. I've been eating it since I was nine years old and I'm still eating today."

Rooi uses a match to scrape the thorns off the branches and hands it to his 44-year-old neighbour, Susanna Witbooi, who says she will crush it into powder to treat her sister's asthma. I ask her what she thinks of the international excitement about the hoodia's hunger-busting properties — the fact that the Viagra pharmaceutical company, Pfizer, is spending millions of dollars using it to create a new dieting drug. She shakes her head and laughs.

For Witbooi the hoodia is just part of life — always has been. "All the San people here use the *xhoba* and in Namibia they even give it to their dogs to eat when they are hungry. In the old days the men often went three days in mid-summer without food or water when they were hunting and they never felt hungry or thirsty, and now it's going to make life better for me and for my children," she says.

The San — or Bushmen as many still prefer to be called — trace their roots in the region back to the first modern humans 150 000 years ago, but the Boers regarded them as vermin and were still organising "Bushman hunts" at the start of the 20th century. Many were forcibly removed from their ancestral lands; others wiped out by European diseases or dislocated by slavery and conflict with African tribes.

Most South African San were classified as coloured under apartheid. They became "farm boys" or "house girls" or were used as South African Defence Force trackers in Namibia. Along the way, their culture was buried. Bushmen cave paintings have been dated at more than 20 000 years old, but the last cave painter died 70 years ago, ending a practice that was integral to their ancestor-based religion. And the ancient Khomani San language also seemed to be dying (with only nine native speakers alive today), replaced by Afrikaans and Nama.

Some San clans in Botswana and Namibia maintain the old way of life, but this seemed on the verge of extinction in South Africa until 1994. Nelson Mandela was particularly proud that his country was home to the world's oldest indigenous culture and his government moved quickly to settle two major land claims that returned large tracts of land to San communities — including the Khomani of the Kalahari, where the best hoodia grows.

Nigel Crawhall, a Canadian linguist who works with the Khomani community, compares their plight with that of Botswana's 55 000 San. "The Botswana government seems embarrassed by the presence of what they regard as a primitive people. They are using force to remove them from their ancestral lands but South Africa took the opposite approach and settled their land claims quickly, with the result that there is now a growing sense of San pride. There are still huge problems related to poverty and dislocation, like widespread alcoholism, HIV/Aids, domestic violence and drug use but people are returning to the land, starting to relearn their traditional languages and to develop a far stronger San identity."

The Khomani San may have been using the hoodia for thousands of years, but for the government's Council for Scientific and Industrial Research (CSIR) it all started in 1963. Its curiosity was inspired by two sources: first, a 1937 research paper from a Dutch ethno-biologist who quoted Khomani hunters on the plant's appetite suppressing qualities; second, information supplied to the military by Khomani San trackers who also used it as a source of water.

The CSIR decided to test the San hunger-busting claims and found they stood up to scrutiny. After a decade-long lull the CSIR resumed its research in the 1980s, and eventually isolated the relevant bioactive compound, and in 1997 patented it as "P57".

The CSIR licensed P57 to the British drug research company Phytopharm, which specialises in trials based on traditional medicines. After conducting double-blind trials (one group taking P57; the other a placebo), Phytopharm confirmed the CSIR's claims and sub-licensed it to the United States pharmaceutical giant, Pfizer, at a price of $21-million. (Incidentally, some San elders chuckle at the Pfizer connection, because they say the hoodia also has Viagra-type properties — or as one put it, "when the grandfathers eat the *xhoba*, the grandmothers can't let them out of their sight").

Meanwhile South Africa's 7 000 San were forging links with other Southern African San communities and forming national and regional councils to represent their interests. The first they heard of the patents was when their solicitor, Roger Chennels, came across a quote from Phytopharm head Dr Richard Dixey, who said that the people who discovered the plant "have disappeared".

Chennels, a 52-year-old human rights lawyer, proudly showed me an intricately designed hunting bow and arrow that took pride of place on his farmhouse-office wall in Stellenbosch. It had been presented to him by a Khomani San leader for his role in winning back their ancestral land — as it happened, shortly before hearing the claim that his clients were "extinct".

He immediately realised this fallacy represented an opportunity and contacted the newly formed San Council, who asserted their rights as the source of the knowledge about the hoodia. "The timing was a complete luck," he acknowledges. "The San have been giving away their secrets for ever, but it was only then that they were in a position to benefit. Any earlier and they might not have been in a position to act on it."

The CSIR acknowledged its mistake: "They realised that if they fought this they'd be in big trouble, so they came to us cap in hand and apologised," says Chennels. Asked to comment, the CSIR insisted it had never claimed the Khomani San were extinct and stressed that its 1998 biopolicy stated that owners of indigenous knowledge "will benefit from commercialisation of research findings". "Meeting up with the San was about implementing our own policy," says CSIR director Dr Petro Terblanche.

In any event the Khomani San had no interest in snubbing these overtures. They realised that a successful patent challenge might lead to open season on the hoodia, with no benefit to the indigenous communities. The best option for both parties therefore lay in negotiation and in February this year, the CSIR and the San Council reached a "memorandum of understanding" acknowledging the rights of the Bushmen as "custodians of the ancient body of traditional knowledge" and the CSIR's role in developing the technology involved in extracting the plant's anti-obesity properties.

There are still crucial loose ends to settle — not least the precise division of future profits — but if Pfizer meets its goal of marketing P57 in 2007, the San hope to receive several million rand a year to be shared between all the San communities within Southern Africa. Chennels has the task of ensuring that the money will be tightly audited in a way that will minimise the risk of corruption and ensure that the communities, rather than a few individuals, will reap the benefits. In the meantime, the CSIR and Phytopharm have agreed that the San will be involved in the cultivation of the plant and will be assisted with bursaries, education programmes, computer training and annual performance payments from 2004.

Dixey, who says he is "embarrassed" by his earlier claim that the Khomani San had disappeared, is delighted that the hoodia's custodians are now firmly on board. "The San-CSIR deal is very far-sighted and I think there's the potential for a happy ending," he says. "One of the main assets of traditional people lies in the wealth of their ancient medical knowledge but it is usually difficult for them to get any payback from this. This case is unusual because the Khomani San were clearly the primordial originators of the knowledge about the hoodia, and they have been able to act on it. This could be the first time ever that a traditional people get royalties from one of their herbs and plants, and while money is obviously part of it, I think they will also be reinforced in their view of life by the international recognition of their way of life."

There is no guarantee P57 will get through the final loop of American Food and Drug Administration approval, but the two companies involved are optimistic it will one day have a major impact in combating obesity. "The trial we conducted last year was extremely impressive," says Dixey. "It showed that P57 reduced appetite by an average of 2 000 calories a day, which is remarkable."

With this kind of data in its bank, Phytopharm has begun setting up hoodia plantations and supply units in South Africa. Pfizer has already spent more than $400-million in additional research, in preparation for its entry into a market currently estimated at more than $3-billion a year in the US alone.

Back in the Kalahari these numbers may still seem remote, but you can sense the spread of a cautious optimism. Men like Rooi are just relieved to be back in the land where the hoodia grows. The past is the past and future will take care of itself. "For most of my life I had to work on white people's farms but now we own our own land. I was born here and I will die here too."

For Witbooi, however, the hoodia deal offers far more: a fresh hope for her children's prospects.

"Things have already improved for me," she says. "I've worked in white people's kitchens in Upington since I was 14 but now at last I am back home, and doing well making crafts for the Khomani craft project. But children like Kayla [her daughter] are the future and they need more, so I feel very grateful that these companies are going to be making pills out of the *xhoba*. I'm hoping the money will bring us teachers and computers and work projects. Things will be much better in the future." **03.01**

Jumbo poo is good for you

Fiona Macleod

Elephants in the Knysna forest are medicating themselves with "magic mushrooms" that could be used by people to counter the effects of HIV. Research shows the elephants are eating a type of mushroom called *Ganoderma applanatum*, a large fungus that grows on trees and can live for up to 50 years. Though it is not hallucinogenic, it is known as a "magic mushroom" because of its healing powers.

Also known as reishi, the mushroom has been used in Asian cultures for thousands of years to promote good health and recuperation. Western medicine has recently woken up to its potential in stimulating the immune system. It is increasingly being used as an anti-inflammatory agent in the treatment of cancer, Alzheimer's and cardiovascular ailments, as well as for treating hypertension, arthritis, bronchitis hepatitis and chronic fatigue syndrome.

Gareth Patterson, who has been tracking the elephants through the forest for the past two years, suggests they are using the fungus to counter toxins in their diet. "The forest vegetation they are eating, including ferns and fynbos, has a high tannin content. Tannin causes liver problems and I am speculating this has something to do with the elephants eating mushrooms."

Patterson's research indicates that Outeniqua communities living around the forest used to drink a tea made out of elephant droppings to boost their immune systems. And a researcher at the University of Mutare in Zimbabwe working with Aids orphans has discovered communities who are using *Ganoderma* to boost their immune systems. "Instead of importing expensive medicines, they are drinking the mushrooms in tea form," says Patterson. He contacted elephant experts in India and East Africa, who said they were unaware of other elephant populations using *Ganoderma*. However, Diane Fossey recorded gorillas using the mushroom for medicinal purposes.

Patterson has been sending elephant dung samples to Lori Eggert, a researcher at the Smithsonian Institution in the United States, for DNA testing. The object is to determine how many elephants there are in the Knysna forest, of what sex and whether there is any chance they will start mating.

Eggert has developed a genetic censusing method using DNA extracted from dung. It was used to determine that the forest elephants of West Africa are genetically distinct from the continent's other two known elephant types, and is providing information needed for the effective management of other declining species around the world.

The Knysna elephants are legendary and mysterious. The only free-ranging elephants in South Africa, their mystique has increased over the years as they seemed to disappear without a trace. Numerous books and films have documented their demise. There were an estimated 100 000 elephants roaming South Africa prior to the arrival of European settlers. By the 1920s ivory traders and hunters had ensured there were only four small pockets of elephants left — and the Southern Cape population, numbering less than 20 elephants in the Knysna forest and what is now the Addo National Park, was the largest.

During the 20th century, the number in the Knysna forest steadily declined until in 1999 an elderly elephant cow named the Matriarch was declared the last Knysna elephant. Efforts to provide her with the company of youngsters translocated from the Kruger park did not work out and they were moved to a private game reserve in the Eastern Cape.

Patterson started searching the Knysna forest after reading about the lonely Matriarch. He has covered hundreds of kilometres on foot in the past two years, and has come to the conclusion that she is not alone. "I am convinced there are three or four elephants out there. The tracks indicate the youngest is about 10 years, there is a female of about 16, a young bull and an adult of possibly 30." Yet he has not found any signs of the Matriarch, who would be about 54 now if she is alive. Patterson and two forestry guards who have also been tracking elephants, Karel Maswati and Wilfred Oraai, believe the Matriarch might be dead.

The results of the DNA research will take a couple of months. Meanwhile, Patterson has taken a leaf out of his subjects' book and is treating his own hypertension with the "magic mushroom". *Ganoderma* is available in various commercial forms, including tablets, extracts, tinctures and teas. It is a multibillion-rand industry in China, where it is considered to be one of the "herbs of the gods" capable of even bringing the dead back to life. Patterson is hoping this belief will be true of the near-extinct Knysna forest elephants. **07.03**

LETTER
Simple science

More than 3 000 elephants face the death sentence — because science has failed to come up with a cheap elephant contraceptive, you tell us. At the risk of sending scientists stampeding for their Minoras, I have mustered some outrage at science's other notable recent failures. No cheap, single-dose anti-retroviral regimen for those living with Aids. No vaccine or cure either, damn it. No cheap way of reversing the greenhouse effect, no practical alternative to fossil fuels. Perhaps we should organise a lynch mob for science. It's obviously failing us terribly. Either that, or we expect too much from it. — *David Le Page, Diep River, 12.09*

True lies or false truths?

David Macfarlane

"The station bomb in 1960 was the first act of urban terrorism in South Africa." True or false?

Well-informed high school students who sweated over this, the first question in last month's History Olympiad paper, must surely have realised they were facing a sticky situation. The vagueness of the phrase "the station bomb" would have knitted some brows, and not even the best-informed of candidates could possibly have identified some such happening in 1960. Hapless candidates who felt sufficiently sure that the question must be referring to the explosion in the Johannesburg railway station for which John Harris was convicted might well have ticked "false", on the reasonable ground that this explosion occurred in 1964, not 1960.

Others might have suppressed some qualms about whether the phrase "urban terrorism" has some widely accepted meaning, and reasoned that a lot in South Africa's history before 1960 could arguably be so described. Incidents during the 1922 white miners' strike, for example, suggests John Pampallis, director of the Centre for Education Policy Development. For these candidates, "false" would also have been their choice. But this was a practice question with the answer sternly supplied: "True." So all these candidates would have been wrong.

Candidates then had to pick their way through the minefield of real questions. They soon encountered this: "During the Seventies President Hastings Banda of Zaire was one of the few African leaders that [sic] was willing to engage in serious dialogue with South Africa." True or false?

Well, false if you prefer to situate the fly-whisking former strongman where he belongs — in Malawi; true if you take the courageously risky step of assuming that the examiners have erred and that "true" is the answer they want. And true too that the English here and elsewhere in the paper leaves a lot to be desired, as several academics commented to the *Mail & Guardian* this week.

The organiser of the Olympiad is the Suid-Afrikaanse Akademie vir Wetenskap en Kuns. Established in 1909, the academy is, according to its (translated) website, a "multi-disciplinary science organisation. Its goals are the promotion of the sciences, technical skills ['tegniek'] and the arts through Afrikaans and the promotion of the use and the quality of the Afrikaans language." The competition is sponsored by The Rhodes Trust. Based at Oxford University, the trust is perhaps best known for its use of Cecil John Rhodes's legacy to fund the prestigious Rhodes Scholarships, awarded since 1903 to students in Britain's former colonies.

Eminent South African historians challenge both the testing method and the apparent ideological leanings of the paper. "While the History Olympiad is supposed to promote history in schools, the paper includes so many errors and distortions that it constitutes a gross disservice to history," says Christopher Saunders, professor of history at the University of Cape Town.

Diverse organisations run the South African Olympiads in a number of school subjects. The competitions are not part of the school curriculum, and have no formal relation with the national or provincial education departments. This year more than 120 schools entered the History Olympiad, and about 1 200 students wrote the first-round paper last month.

"I am surprised," Minister of Education Kader Asmal told the M&G after perusing the question paper this week, "that The Rhodes Trust has anything to do with a history approach that is firmly entrenched in the Christian National Education system of the past, which has nothing to do with our new conception of education and the place of history in a democratic South Africa."

Dr Wessel Visser, a historian at the University of Stellenbosch who chaired the seven-member panel that set the questions, told the *M&G*: "I concede mistakes occur from time to time. But people mustn't get the idea there's an ideological agenda here. We're not approaching history from any angle. The academy might have had ideological agendas in the past, but not now."

"The paper is a huge mess," says Emilia Potenza, author of history textbooks and a history curriculum policy developer. "It encourages the worst approach to teaching history, as though it's merely a matter of facts — often highly dubious facts in this paper. In history, there's not always consensus — there are debates and interpretations. It's exactly here that history in the new school curriculum locates itself, and so raises critical questions such as whose version of history do we hear, what constitutes evidence and reliability, and how does one marshal evidence to build an argument. These are valuable cognitive skills — crucial to building society and democracy — that are completely undermined by the Olympiad's approach."

Educationally, the questions "reflect a disastrous frame of mind", says Professor Jeff Guy, the University of Natal historian and author of *The Destruction of the Zulu Kingdom*. "What killed history in the past was its insistence on an uncreative memorising of facts. The paper's attitude to knowledge reflects the state of history as taught in the apartheid era, with its authoritarian commitment to the memory of facts." **06.04**

Neither saint nor saviour

Jaspreet Kindra

Now that the dust around the Truth and Reconciliation Commission (TRC) report has settled, the reputation of former president FW de Klerk's legacy as a peacemaker and a co-liberator is being reassessed. The final report castigates De Klerk's snubbing of its process, and this week a former TRC commissioner joined TRC chairperson Archbishop Desmond Tutu and senior former National Party members in painting a less sanguine picture of the former president.

Tutu's autobiography, *No Future without Forgiveness*, slates De Klerk, saying that he should have withheld endorsement for De Klerk's Nobel Peace Prize. De Klerk, now a speaker on the international statesman's circuit, insists his reputation has not been tarnished, and he continues to blame a loaded TRC for painting him in an uncomplimentary light. At issue for the TRC is De Klerk's refusal to acknowledge his and the Nats' responsibility for the gross human rights violations that took place under the apartheid regime.

TRC commissioner Yasmin Sooka said this week: "We [the TRC] had great expectations from De Klerk, a Nobel Peace Prize-winner, who unlike PW Botha had crossed the Rubicon and would avail himself of the magnanimous opportunity offered to all white South Africans."

The TRC, in its final two volumes released two weeks ago, cites international law, including the First Additional Protocol to the Geneva Conventions of 1949 and the International Criminal Tribunal for the former Yugoslavia. These state that any acts committed by subordinates do not relieve their superiors of criminal responsibility. Sooka says this section was written with reference to the NP governments that oversaw the apartheid order.

The TRC report describes as "indefensible" De Klerk's statement before the commission in 1996 that none of his colleagues in the Cabinet, the State Security Council or Cabinet committees had authorised assassination, murder or other gross violation of human rights. The finding was made in relation to the bombing of Khotso House.

Tutu wrote in his memoirs that when the Norwegian Nobel committee telephoned him for his opinion on their intention to award the 1993 Nobel Peace Prize jointly to Nelson Mandela and De Klerk, he had supported the decision enthusiastically. Tutu writes: "Had I known then what I know now, I would have opposed it vehemently."

De Klerk's refusal to admit responsibility was glaring in the face of the testimony given by his former colleagues and members of the State Security Council. Those who testified before the commission included former NP minister of law and order Adriaan Vlok, minister of foreign affairs Pik Botha and deputy justice minister Leon Wessels. De Klerk's failure to follow in his colleagues' footsteps caused Tutu to remark: "He was incapable of seeing apartheid for what it was — intrinsically evil. He is a very bright lawyer who qualifies his answers carefully to protect his position, but in doing this he has steadily eroded his stature, becoming in the process a small man, lacking magnanimity and generosity of spirit. I hope he has the sensitivity to realise that his idea of establishing an institute for reconciliation, which he announced in 1998, would rub salt into the wounds of the victims of a policy over which he presided."

Tutu's remarks are the most severe pall over De Klerk's legacy, though his former colleague, Roelf Meyer, says his decision in 1990 to begin dismantling apartheid was a historic moment. Meyer says history cannot deny De Klerk credit for having begun the dismantling of apartheid, but says the leader did not really undertake the "paradigm shift" that power should vest in the hands of the majority. Meyer says the Nats who decided to appear before the TRC of their own accord were unhappy with De Klerk's written submission to the commission. "I did not agree with his approach, which is why I made my own submission, and by that time I had already been sacked by him."

After 1994, De Klerk's progressive political will seemed to seep away, and he actively opposed efforts to transform the NP. Meyer explains that before 1994 De Klerk was the state president, and with the position came the authority with which he could shut down voices of dissent from the conservative elements within the NP.

Throughout the negotiations, says Meyer, De Klerk fought for the conservative elements within the NP to support him. "I remember when Nelson Mandela was released, De Klerk said to me, 'We are now starting with the liquidation of the old regime' — that to my mind was a very clear statement about his commitment to change."

Yet in 1997 it was De Klerk who turned down Botha's proposal that the entire former Nat Cabinet apply for amnesty. Botha recalls that when the ANC leaders decided to apply for amnesty, he wrote a letter to De Klerk in 1997: "I reasoned with him that since the ANC was doing it we would stand out like a *seer duim* [sore thumb]. I said if he takes the lead with all the ex-Cabinet ministers, it would also help in the reconciliation between the ANC and the NP." It was shot down by the conservative elements within the party, with whom De Klerk concurred.

De Klerk this week denied that his legacy is questionable. His spokesperson, Dave Steward, says: "The whole theme and purpose of Mr de Klerk's presidency was the systematic dismantling of all the remaining apartheid laws, culminating finally in the negotiation of a new non-racial and fully democratic constitution." He said the former Nat leader "could not accept — and was under no obligation to accept — responsibility for actions that were taken in express contravention of his instruction, and were aimed at undermining the policies of transformation that he himself had initiated".

The TRC, Steward says, has chosen to ignore the "sincere apology" that De Klerk made for all the human rights violations caused by apartheid. Steward claims the TRC was biased against the NP and wished to impose its own "struggle" version of the past. He says: "It also became clear that the TRC — and particularly the staffers on the commission — were determined to do as much damage as possible to De Klerk's reputation presumably because of their view that nothing good or honourable could possibly come from the past."

He also refutes Meyer's observations that De Klerk was not prepared for majority rule. He points out that since it was De Klerk who had initiated the transformation process in 1990, he was well aware the process would lead to majority rule — though De Klerk has subsequently issued withering critiques of majoritarianism. "The majoritarian reality, which has now, to a certain extent, been thrust on us, contains the clear threat of the kind of racial domination which must be avoided at all costs," he says in his autobiography, *The Last Trek: A New Beginning.*

Steward points out that De Klerk established the Goldstone commission and the Steyn investigation to "uncover evidence of wrongdoing" involving the security forces. But journalist Allister Sparks, in his book *Tomorrow Is Another Country,* says De Klerk made "half-hearted attempts to clamp down on the renegade elements in his security forces" after the investigations found evidence of third-force activity.

How should De Klerk go down in history? The jury's still out, but on balance, the view from the most influential quarters of South Africa is that his history is that of a political pragmatist and a man whose hand was forced by circumstance rather than by principle. Many have criticised the TRC for various reasons, but De Klerk's snubbing of it went further than most — he took them to court twice and continues to cast aspersions on its constitution. A question the Nobel Peace Prize committee should perhaps ask itself is one being asked in many South African quarters: did we act in haste? **04.04**

A world gone crazy

Athelé Wills

I'm just back from an extensive tour around the United States and am left grappling with the unshakeable impression that I live in a world gone stark raving mad. Look at the facts:

● The combined national economies of the poorest 48 countries are way below the assets of the three richest people in the world.

● One-fifth of the people in the world eke out an existence on a dollar or less a day, while a whole chunk of the rest suffer from symptoms of excess, like obesity (which affects 33% of Americans).

The world has to be declared mad, institutionalised and put into intensive care for emergency healing. Now.

It's what some nations were trying to do at the World Summit on Sustainable Development in Jo'burg. I remember wondering how President George W Bush was explaining the US's lack of concern to his voters. After our brief immersion in American culture it became very clear.

Here's the thing — his countrymen don't know. Most of them are too deep in a trance. Yes, it's a sweeping statement and there are exceptions. But I'm talking about the average American, almost any one of the 280-odd million folk who make up the "land of the free and home of the brave".

Here's where the hint of evil emerges — you feed them only what you want them to know. And a once-great nation of people is brainwashed into becoming a compliant herd of sheep-like, voracious consumers.

Seven weeks in the US translated into seven weeks of not knowing what was going on in the world. Sure, information is available to the dedicated world-watcher. But unless you go out and look for it, you're only going to get news about the US.

That's why most of my family and friends in the US knew nothing about the World Summit — even though it was under way as my husband and I boarded the plane for Chicago out of Johannesburg International.

I fully anticipated the US's embarrassing position at the summit to be a hot topic of conversation at my birthday party in Cincinnati two nights later. Not so. In fact it hadn't even impinged on their consciousness. And I wasn't going to be the one to broach it. It seemed uncouth to talk about the US's pivotal role in the destruction of our home while I nibbled on the snacks so kindly brought by my sister-in-law's guests.

When I found myself standing in her kitchen at the end of the party scraping mountains of untouched food into the bin I couldn't resist murmuring something about it paining me terribly, since I know the village I live next door to in Africa is in a daily battle to keep the kwashiorkor wolf from the door. "I know. Waste in America is really terrible," was the response of my fellow cleaner. "But what can you do about it? That's the system here," she said sadly, but categorically, and in closing.

I could suddenly see why, at first hand, Bush and his policies — while making unwelcome waves across the world — failed to create the smallest ripple in the consciousness of his people. Those who care feel locked in the system, unable to sustain even the smallest voice.

What do you do when a company as pervasive as Subway, serving billions of stuffed rolls a day across the US, has its staff handing out a great wedge of "napkins" with every roll. Do you carefully stack them in a cupboard to use later? No way — you'd need a spare garage to cope with them.

So you toss them, along with one-third of your uneaten Subway, in the bin. The sad thing is, it won't take long before you do it without a backward glance. And so you become an active participant in the death of the planet — without even thinking about it. Because you'll almost certainly have a chunk of your vastly over-stuffed foot-long Subway to throw away. It will be overstuffed because it costs the same whether you have all of the 20 options crammed into your Subway or not. And who would buy a six-inch roll for $3,29 when a foot-long only costs $1,70 extra? So the choice you land up with is to get fat, or throw food away.

Which brings me to another way the evil of over-consumerism has insidiously bored its way into the mind of the US's purchasing public. Its aggressive marketing system, funded by the over-rich multi-national corporations (MNCs), convinces you that it never pays to buy less. More is more in the US. Buy one, it costs you $4. Buy a second one and you can have them both for $6,20. But if we can tempt you to make the massive saving of buying a dozen, you can have them all for $19,99. Obviously you would be a fool to buy one.

And so it comes to pass that 20% of the world's population is stick thin, dying of starvation, Aids and preventable diseases ... while the 20% at the other end of the scale is eating up 80% of the world's resources, commanding most of its money, and dying of obesity, cancer, heart disease, diabetes and strokes. What's thrown in trash cans across the US daily could make the difference between empty pot bellies and healthy bodies across great swathes of Africa.

Those obese Americans, girding their considerable loins to challenge fast-food giants to hold them liable for their condition, are barking up the wrong tree. They should be banding together with all their fellow citizens, lobbying government to overhaul the runaway marketing machine that fuels the problem. For marketers have virtual carte blanche in the US. Even governments cannot act against the interests of the MNCs and the international money industry out of fear of capital flight making a mockery of democracy. Farcical, isn't it?

Aggression is an understatement for the way in which marketers in the US go about persuading consumers to over-consume. It's a no-holds-barred affair. They press you into applying for buying cards that give "massive savings" for store loyalty (read: penalise you if you don't). Sell you a brand-new motor vehicle that you don't have to pay any interest on or even make any payments on for more than a year. Then when all the chickens come home to roost and you find that your monthly earnings are swallowed by the 15 stores' charge cards and the car payments that you'd long-since forgotten, why, then there's the debt consolidator who can just magic all those nightmares away. Now you only have one creditor. Who keeps you in his grip beyond the end of your days, extracting your final sum owed plus 30 years' interest accumulated from the scraps you'd otherwise have had to offer your heirs.

No wonder Americans work long hours and companies generally only offer two weeks' leave a year. Small wonder they don't travel overseas in their droves — by the time the American marketer is finished with you, there's nothing left. Which is exactly the way the MNCs would have it. The way the world's economic system is currently set up depends massively on the over-consumptive habits of

Americans. The irony that passes over the heads of these very consumers is that two-thirds of them face heightened risks of cancer because of exposure to toxins ingested in all the junk food they are forever stuffing down their throats.

That's another crazy note in the discordant symphony; for all their efforts to protect their farmers and all their industrialisation and progress, American food tastes hollow. Why is this? Mostly because of inappropriate land use and the perceived need for genetically modifying their produce. Another symptom of the madness. Industrialised nations currently spend $360-billion annually on subsidising farmers, a sum recently inflated even further by Bush.

This was another sticking point at the summit — as the Third World begged, without success, for an entry into the world food-producing market. This status quo serves the powers that be. Ditto the whole crazy issue of fossil fuels that is fuelling the US's next war in the Middle East. It is a case of the arms and the fossil-fuel industry sustaining each other. Whatever their motives, even we found petrol cheap in the US, albeit our rand was 11 to the dollar at the time. Small wonder most of America ride around in gas-guzzling cars.

You see, that's the thing. It's there, it's super-comfortable and super-easy, and so everyone just goes along with it. Even while the pundits are telling us that unless fossil-fuel use slows dramatically, the Earth's average temperature could rise by 6°C within the next 100 years. Which scientists agree spells disaster for all.

But the current economic model is driven by fossil fuels. Albeit suicidal. One morning in Phoenix we caught a Sky Couriers kombi to the airport. Our driver told us his van was kitted out to run off propane gas. It had already done well over 800 000km and looked set to do the same again. There's almost no wear on the engine; your oil goes out the same way it came in, clean. Propane also has water as a by-product, cutting harmful emissions to zero. It costs about the same to run his kombi on propane gas as it would on petrol, he told us. And yet his specially modified vehicle was probably less than one in a million of the cars on the highway that morning. It doesn't suit anyone making policy decisions to usher out petrol-driven vehicles just yet.

But would Americans, given the chance to do something to make a difference, cooperate anyway? We flew by the rest of the traffic, ground to virtual standstill in the morning rush hour. That's because we were in the seventh lane — the one that insists on more than one passenger. We had it virtually to ourselves.

That's the really sad part. There are efforts being made, albeit by a small minority. My sister-in-law diligently recycles her paper, glass and plastics. She has a wonderfully efficient recycling company that collects on a regular basis.

It's a documented fact that most materials in industrial nations are discarded after being used once only. Yet harmful emissions from factories are largely to blame for the fact that the 1990s were the hottest decade since measurements began in the 19th century. Sea levels have risen nearly 20cm in the past 100 years.

My friend Mary, in upstate New York, is also keenly aware of the ills of her society. She does all she can to prevent waste. But she despairs much of the time and feels like an inaudible voice being swept away in a hurricane of consumption.

She knows that the National Academy of Sciences in Washington warned that the consumption of forests, energy and land by humans now exceeds the rate at which the Earth can replenish itself. That it takes the Earth 1,2 years to regenerate what people remove every year. But she also knows that her fellow countrymen are too caught up in the American dream to wake up and smell the last vestiges of coffee as they drift out the window of opportunity forever.

Ever the optimist, I reminded her of the power of one. Consider that the cost of implementing the Millennium Development Goals (which aim to halve the world's poverty by 2015) is between $50-billion and $100-billion a year. If the developed nations of the world had met their commitment from a decade ago — to provide 0,7% of their gross domestic product for development aid — we would have that amount and change every year.

But to get that to happen is going to take pressure from within. I have great hope. But then I come from a land where I witnessed at first hand how the will of the people prevails. And at this point in time the will of the American people to break out of their complacency and comfort-zone is clearly sadly lacking.

It seems, for now, that it's up to the rest of the world to change first. Then drag them with us, kicking and screaming if needs be. Whoever suggested that South Africa should hold the American way of life up as a role model was caught up in the illusion so skilfully portrayed by the machine.

Let's just make sure we all stay with the facts and do what we can in our lives to continue to lead the world into a new way of being that will sustain us into an indefinite future. **10.01**

Athelé Wills is a Limpopo-based freelance journalist

LETTERS

American nightmare

Having lived in the United States for just over a year, I can identify with Athelé Wills. Far from being a dream, the US turns most citizens into brainwashed, ignorant, bored over-consumers. The system is geared towards maximum inactivity, instant gratification and spending most of one's life in a car.

Television gives zero information on the rest of the world, unless the US military is involved; political debates are a farce; the length and number of commercials is maddening.

Motorways are clogged with gas-guzzling monsters carrying one passenger on average, while rudimentary public transport is underused. There is no need for the slightest hunger pang, as there is a fast food joint at every off-ramp. Most suburbs do not have pavements; roads are built through every forest, reserve and park. Lakes are not places of peace, but of torturous exposure to ear-deafening jet skis and motor boats. Swimming in a lake invites surprise.

The amount of junk mail one receives every day can keep you busy for hours. Large chain stores, their characterless warehouses with concrete car-parks stretching to the horizon, take over everything. Don't expect vibrant flea markets such as Rosebank Rooftop or Greenmarket Square.

My spirit underwent major upliftment as I touched down on South African soil. — *Dr Y Reister, Johannesburg, 24.01*

There's no place like home

I wish to congratulate Athelé Wills for her very succinct account of the American way of life. Having spent just over two years in the United States, I cannot wait to go back home. Give me South African whingeing and bickering any day. The degree of ignorance and insularity in the US is unimaginable; people are too caught up in their consumerism to care about what their political representatives are up to. And, as Wills points out, the few who do care face almost insurmountable obstacles as they are casually branded unpatriotic and pushed to the periphery of the political debate.

A case in point is the current Iraq debacle. Even though thousands have marched in protest against the war in almost all major cities, none of the news organisations has carried a rigorous analysis of what really lies behind the seemingly unstoppable march to war. Most coverage seems to assume that the war is a foregone conclusion; most of the analysis is already on the nature of a post-Saddam Iraq.

South Africa, with all its problems, is still a great place to live in. Just browsing through a few of our newspapers and listening to our radio talk shows illustrate that we are a nation in conversation with ourselves. Even as we bicker about the nature of our ills and tribulations, this is still a manifestation of our love for country. There is little of the nauseating "flag-waving herd mentality" that seems to have overtaken the US since September 11. To all those who think emigration is the answer — it's not always greener on the other side. — *Loyiso Pulumani, Connecticut, United States, 17.01*

The grass *is* greener on the other side

As a South African citizen who lived in the United States for three months, I would like to comment about the "American nightmares" your letter writer J Reister referred to. I feel I must respond since very few black women from South Africa travel to the US and my experiences were very different.

I'm surprised when he says the television gives no information on the rest of the world. I watched the news and I got everything I wanted to know about South Africa, even the bomb blast in my home town of Soweto.

I found transport easy because you don't spend your time standing in queues waiting to be squashed like sardines in a bus or a taxi. Reister's comment that there is no place to walk is wrong — there are many places and they are safe. And parks are the safest places to go, unlike here, where a guy I know was robbed of R500 and his cellphone at Zoo Lake.

There is no crime in the US like here. In the US I forgot that I was black, as I was treated like a queen — which would never happen here. Please South Africans, let us all be equal!

Why are so many South African moving to the US? To Americans that come to South Africa I say: we love you. — *Beauty Mtolo, Freedom Park, 07.02*

Lessons from imperial history

Jeff Guy

One of the weapons historians use to defend their discipline from the ill-disciplined hordes from commerce, computer and media studies is a banner with the slogan "To understand the present we must understand the past". I've tried this tactic myself — and have been bowled, banner and all, into the gutter as battalions of first-years head for the computers and move, as their counter-slogans say, "Into the future".

And yet increasingly over the past few months, as the latest world crisis moves towards war, it is not the future but history, the tragic and terrifying past, of which I am reminded. It is time for history to reclaim and regain its place as the discipline not only of the past, but of the future. Let's look at an event from South Africa's past. Onehundred and twenty years ago the most powerful country in the world came to the conclusion that it should force a change in the geopolitics of a distant part of the world in which it had an interest. It was time, this great power felt, to bring progress to the region. If this meant removing some of the less progressive individuals and states from the equation — well, who could object to the march of civilisation and of Christianity?

The most powerful country was, of course, Great Britain. The obstacle to the plan to bring about a unified, progressive, capitalist South Africa was the Zulu kingdom under Cetshwayo kaMpande. How was the plan carried out? First the argument had to be individualised — it is easier to hate a person than a people — and a case was devised against the Zulu king. The press and MPs in London were fed reports showing that Cetshwayo was a cruel despot. His people yearned to be released from the tyranny of his rule. His army was a "celibate man-slaying machine" that posed a threat to peace and progress in South Africa. He was in contact with other African leaders, urging them to resist white rule and restore the idle savagery of traditional Africa. The safety and security of South Africa, it was argued, depended on the removal of the Zulu king, and thousands of British troops were ordered to the borders of the Zulu kingdom to prepare for this.

But not everyone agreed that war was necessary. A commission was set up to examine the boundary dispute between the Zulu and the Boers — and it found in favour of the Zulu. The finding was not made public. Instead an ultimatum was drawn up: if the Zulu king did not disband his army within 30 days, then the British army would do so by force. Of course it was known that the Zulu king would never abandon his sovereignty. In January 1879 the British invaded the Zulu kingdom.

It is all so reminiscent of what is happening today in the plans to invade Iraq. I am not, of course, arguing that the historical links are direct: a Zulu king is not like an Iraqi dictator; and the reasons that those who rule the United States need to control the Middle East today are not the same as those that drove Britain to gain control of South Africa more than a century ago. But if we step back from these events and take the broader perspective, then the landscape becomes familiar — it is the landscape of imperialism.

And this is what we see. A distant, sovereign state gets in the way of the plans of a world power to extend its interests. In order to get rid of this nuisance it is decided to use war to bring about regime change. Of course this can't be said openly, so a great moral purpose — freedom for the oppressed — is invoked. The media are fixed, allies are bribed, attempts at peace are subverted, an individual is depicted as the epitome of evil. Massive numbers of troops are moved into the region and an ultimatum is drawn up to provide the pretext for war.

It is such themes that link the imperial past with events in the contemporary world. It is these imperatives — when those with power use moral arguments to justify their destruction of the less powerful — that characterise so many imperial wars. It is these themes that the British invasion of the Zulu kingdom of 1879, and the intended invasion of Iraq today, have in common. And it is these shared themes that give me the confidence to write on my banner the embattled historians' slogan: "To understand the present we must understand the past".

And my confidence in history extends further. If I am correct in suggesting that, despite the enormous differences in specific details, it is still possible to use imperial wars of the past to understand the imperial wars of the present, then it might also be possible to use the past to gain some insight into what's going to come. Let's look at what happened in the Zulu kingdom after the invasion began. Firstly, the invading force's modern military technology — rifles, machine guns, artillery and rockets — inflicted terrible casualties on men armed with assegais. Then there was the damage that occupation by an invading army did to the non-combatants — the women, the children and the aged. In the end the Zulu terminated their military resistance to limit this collateral damage. They surrendered, the king was exiled and the victors divided the country among those who had opposed the old order. Civil war broke out: various forces sitting on the ex-kingdom's borders moved in to get hold of what pieces were left. The result? The Zulu lost their independence, their autonomy, the products of their labour and their land. It has never been recovered.

So the lessons to be learned from imperial history are severe. Once the war plan goes into action dreadful suffering will be visited on the people in whose name the war is waged. They will then be liberated from despotic rule: a liberation that will prove hollow as the new rulers fight for their share of the spoils. There can be no democracy: democracy is too difficult to manipulate. The people in whose name the war was waged will lose again — just as the people of the Zulu kingdom lost the moment they were liberated by the British from the despotic rule of their king.

The lessons from history about the future are therefore gloomy, dreadfully gloomy: victory for cultural arrogance, media spin, lies, for those who already possess by far the greatest holdings of the world's weapons of mass destruction, the further suffering of a people who have already suffered more than enough. But we can't leave it at that and there is a third slogan that those who believe in the importance of history like to use. It is one that carries a warning: "Unless we understand the mistakes of the past we are condemned to repeat them."

And here there is a suggestion that we are learning at last; a hint that we are beginning to understand something about the history of imperial power, about the use of force in the making of our global world, about the lies propagated in pursuit of Western civilisation. The hopeless inadequacy of the men and women pursuing war in the Middle East, the transparency of their diplomatic manoeuvring, has become apparent to the people of the world, and millions are coming to realise that the imperial process has to be halted.

On February 15 the ordinary people of the world went on to the streets to show their opposition to this latest imperial adventure. It was the largest popular demonstration in the history of the world. We often hear how the global economy is made possible by the instant movement of capital. Now the people of the globalised world are on the move. At last we have not just an empire, but protest at empire, upon which the sun never sets. The struggle for people's rights, for democracy, for the end of the system of lies and deceit by which the global few rule the global many, is only just beginning. The disparities in power and control remain immense. Our understanding of the way in which imperialism has worked against popular aspirations has yet to be developed and spread.

A closer examination of what happened in the South African past, of how the exercise of imperial violence shaped South Africa, does enable us to understand the present more clearly through the past. Hopefully, we will also be able to use this understanding to avoid repeating past mistakes. For, in spite of the obvious differences, it is still possible to discern in the preparations being made for war today, the echoes of other imperial wars, like the war that was made on the Zulu kingdom, so long ago in terms of years, and yet so close to us in terms of the broad objectives of those who prosecuted it, and the methods they used. We have to find ways to stop it happening yet again, to anyone, anywhere. **07.03**

Jeff Guy is professor of historical studies at the University of Natal, Durban, author of The Destruction of the Zulu Kingdom, *and a member of Minister of Education Kader Asmal's ministerial history committee*

A war of whores

Mondli Makhanya

So there's going be a war. So there's going to be regime change in Baghdad. So there's going to be lots of "collateral damage" in the form of thousands of dead Arabs. So what?

The world's proud, only and unfettered superpower has deemed that it be so and it shall be so. United States President George W Bush tells us this war is about making the world a safer place, about bringing democracy and freedom to the oppressed people of Iraq, about removing from the Middle East a man who gives succour to international terrorists and keeps dangerous toys in his bottom drawer.

His opponents tell us it is about Bush's need to satisfy the urges of that humungous erection that is the American military, about the need to placate the petroleum giants whose avaricious eyes are on the Iraqi oil fields and about the desire to inject life into a stagnant American economy. But none of those answers tell us why Britain's Tony Blair is such an enthusiastic backer of this destructive mission and why so many other nations have been willing to join the Bush coalition.

The truth is that this is essentially a war of whores. With all due deference to his esteemed office, Bush is a whore who, more than any of his 52 predecessors, has prostituted himself to his country's industrial interests. Yes, Oliver Stone and other conspiracy theorists have said so much about the stranglehold of the military-industrial complex as to discredit the notion. But the reality is that there is a greater power that controls the White House and that power is not the being whose blessing Americans so nonchalantly request each time they want to bomb a small nation.

The greatest weakness of the American model of democracy — and one that we in this part of the world should eschew — is the inordinate influence wielded by business interests and the Washington lobby establishment over elected officials. So this is not necessarily Bush's war. He is just a whore fulfilling the desires of those who control his government.

By the same token, it is not Blair's war either. The British prime minister, a man who a few years ago was a poster boy of the world's New Left, has found himself unable to say no to Bush. So dazzled by American power is Blair that he has allowed his philosophy of a Third Way to fall off the agenda. Instead he has whored himself to the American establishment, allowing himself to be used to legitimise a war that will surely go down as one of the most avoidable conflicts in human history.

More than Saddam Hussein, it will be Blair who will be the worst victim of the regime change that will befall many world leaders as populations vote out those leaders who took them into a war they did not want. Discarded by his people, his party and his European peers, Blair will leave the political stage a soiled man — and *sans* the legacy he so deserved.

A fulfilled Bush will zip up and walk away triumphantly, in search of more whores to exploit in his quest to entrench American domination over humanity. For that is what happens to whores. That is exactly what happened to Saddam when he allowed himself to be used by Bush's predecessors in the war against Iran, the then archevil. Once the US was done with him, Saddam became just another Antichrist in the eyes of the Washington establishment.

That is what happened to the dozens of client states and puppet presidents that the US administration has used and discarded over the decades. And that is what would have happened to the other would-be whores — those countries that were prepared to sell their principles for a fistful of dollars had the issue gone to a vote at the United Nations Security Council.

Tragically, it is not only the global political infrastructure that is being destroyed by this war and American dominance of international affairs. An even worse casualty is the morality of decision-making institutions: the presidencies and parliaments of the world. No longer is there pretence that the world is divided along ideological lines, as was the case in the days when the Soviet Union counterbalanced the US's superpower status. Today the world is divided into those who are prepared to prostitute themselves to the US (whether for money or short-term political gain) and those who aren't.

That is not the way the New World Order which emerged from the rubble of the Cold War was supposed to be. The world we sought to create was one that would build on the foundations of the multilateral institutions that were crafted at the end of World War II. It was a world where humanity would live by civilised rules. It was a world in which the world's wealthy would care about the world's poor and the world's developed nations would do their damnedest to drag the underdeveloped nations out of their quagmire. Conflicts would be solved through multilateral institutions and wars would be embarked upon only when recognised international forums deemed them justifiable.

No. Nobody was so naive as to believe that we would love each other and be one big happy family. But we sure would try. But all those dreams have dissipated now as we plunge into an era when all that matters is the size of your weapon, the bulk of your wallet and the willingness of someone to lie on their backs and shut their eyes.
20.03

LETTERS
A reckless, criminal disregard for life

What this criminal war on Iraq reveals to me is that the United States regards people who do not agree with it as mildly tolerated entities on a planet we all have an equal stake in. Effectively, the US administration has made a decision for the whole world that it has not been mandated to make. Who knows what the world will look like on the other side of this war?

Those who condone this war, talking in clinical terms such as "regime change" and "military strategy", are basically saying that this reckless, criminal disregard for life is okay. People will die, in large numbers and in brutal circumstances. But it seems like the war-hungry among us don't care about this. They talk about collateral damage as though it's the most natural thing in the world. Collateral damage means violent death for those who are not responsible for their country's policies.

People have been saying that the loss of life won't be great. What is "not great" in your books? Is it 10, 1 500, 100 000? Think of the death of someone you love, think of losing your own life. Then talk about "not great". For the people of Iraq, this will not be an academic discussion. Yes, perhaps Saddam Hussein's time is up. But how many innocent victims of this war have to go with him? — *Tebogo Mogale, Johannesburg*

Shades of Neville Chamberlain and "peace in our time"! If Hitler had been timeously dealt with, the occupation of Sudetenland and Poland, World War II and the Holocaust might very well have been avoided.

The millions of people in the United Kingdom, US and elsewhere, marching against the war on Iraq, may yet be grateful for the coalition's unpopular decision to launch a pre-emptive strike against Saddam. I believe history will record such action as crucial to prevent the murderous tyrant from using his weapons of mass destruction against the West, as he has already done against hundreds of thousands of his own citizens, killing Kurds, Shiites and members of the Ba'ath Party.

That Dr Hans Blix and the United Nations did not find VX, racine and anthrax in Iraq is hardly surprising, considering how easy it must have been to hide these poisonous substances in small containers somewhere in the vast area that Iraq encompasses. As for the larger undiscovered missiles, it is my guess that they have been spirited away across the border into Syria. — *Helen Suzman*

One of the incomprehensible things about the war on Iraq is how some apparently intelligent world leaders (most specifically, Tony Blair) have gone along with the Bush rhetoric, which has been long on belligerence and short on logic. Sure, Saddam is a horrible dictator — but what connection does this have with the "war on terror"? The connection has not been established at all, let alone tenuously.

After Afghanistan, how can anyone take Bush's rhetoric about "liberating" Iraq seriously? I haven't met anyone who does, even if Blair, John Howard and Tony Leon do — they are fortunately not in my circle of acquaintances.

Remember the talk about a "Marshall Plan" for Afghanistan? In his 2003 Budget, Bush actually forgot to allocate any aid to Afghanistan ($300-million was added when Congress intervened). Contrast this with more than $10-billion that was justified up front for the war in that country. War with Iraq will likely cost significantly more. I've seen estimates ranging from $50-billion to more than $100-billion. It is conceivable that the war with Iraq wouldn't have been necessary had Bush honoured his commitment to rebuild Afghanistan, and thereby deflated the claim that the US is an anti-Muslim warmongering imperialist regime.

What would it have cost to rebuild Afghanistan? The World Bank has estimated that mine clearance alone would cost over $500-million, more than the entire amount Congress added to correct the omission from the Budget. The overall cost estimated by the World Bank, UN agencies and the Asian Development Bank is $15-billion over the next 10 years. Contrast this with war on Iraq. The US Congressional Budget Office has estimated that the cost of deploying military forces to Iraq alone would be $9-billion to $13-billion.

In other words, just getting its troops to Iraq has cost the US almost as much as it would cost to rebuild Afganistan. Add on the cost of the war — not to mention all the human suffering and the new recruits to the cause of disgruntled extremist Islam — and you have to wonder what the Bush administration's priorities are. — *Philip Machanick, Australia, 28.03*

Don't whine about the bully

The prevailing topics of discussion surrounding Iraq seem tediously linked with the ethics of the invasion and the United States's apparent callousness in dealing with world opinion. Excuse me for thinking it's all a bit irrelevant. The US is the most powerful economic, political and cultural force on the planet. American consumerism has already invaded homes across the globe and destroyed traditions and ideologies that existed for thousands of years.

The US's invasion of Iraq was not an aggressive change in foreign policy. President George W Bush has merely politicised a policy that has dominated US economic strategies for decades: use your power to eliminate any opposition you encounter. If this practice has been so widely accepted in the economic sector, why should it be criticised when employed in the political sphere? What can we do about it?

If the school bully takes your best friend's lunch money, there's no point in whining to him that it's not fair. Accept it and concentrate on making sure he doesn't pick on you. — *Riaz Arbi, Grahamstown, 02.05*

Show us, Helen

Helen Suzman said before the Iraqi invasion she believed Iraq possessed weapons of mass destruction "concealed in scattered hideaways in the vast Iraqi desert, or spirited across the border into Syria". This after exhorting the United States to "go in and finish the job" and saying US bombs would not hit civilian targets.

It would only be fair for Suzman to take US President George W Bush and British Prime Minister Tony Blair into her confidence by showing them where the missing weapons are, relieving them of the danger of having to resign for treasonably taking their countries to war on false pretences. — *Cornwell Ndlovu, Doornfontein, 08.08*

Wanted: Comical Ali

Tom Eaton

Thirty days ago nobody had heard of Mohammed Saeed al-Sahaf. Today everybody has a favourite "Comical Ali" one-liner. The Iraqi minister of information has spawned a T-shirt boom, websites and fan clubs. And why wouldn't he? He is a gem, and one South African sport badly needs.

Imagine what otherworldly observations came from the minister during his inevitable flight to Damascus along with the rest of the Iraqi high command. "Do not be afraid of that helicopter gunship heading for our truck, comrades, any moment now loyal peasants will annihilate it with well-aimed rocks. That is not a missile coming our way, brothers, it is a burning American airman. See how he roars past and slams into the Volvo behind us. While there is nothing to fear, I think we should entrench ourselves behind that patriotic dune over there as I think I see another burning American airman coming our way. Bugger."

It's safe to assume Al-Sahaf's career as a minister is over, but it is almost certain that his creative genius will not be lost to the world. At this moment headhunters from KPMG and Microsoft are racing the marines to the Syrian border in a desperate bid to capture the rarefied mind that steams under that little black beret.

And South African sport has fumbled the ball by not being part of that race. Instead of enlisting the services of the greatest spin doctor since Pik Botha, our sporting leaders continue in the naive belief that the public wants to hear the truth. Signs of this horrible candour are everywhere. Last weekend Stormers captain Corné Krige told news agencies that his team "threw away" their Super 12 match against the Queensland Reds. Good God, Corné, are you mad?

Drunk on this heady mix of defeatism and honesty, coach Gert Smal weighed in with the observation that if one doesn't perform on the day, "you can be humiliated". Oh for two tranquilliser darts and a big black van to carry the unconscious duo away for re-education ... It could have been so lovely. With Krige and Smal chained to each other in a dank cellar under Newlands, Al-Sahaf would have addressed the media. "What appeared to be a Stormers loss was in fact a tactical repositioning of our players. We have found glory by outsmarting the Australian invaders. Their bellies are roasting in hell."

How, some cynically unsporting reporters will ask, do you account for the score? "Naturally the score is a fabrication of the Australian media. There is no score. You are a victim of your country's obsession with scores. Do not panic. I am here. You can call me Al."

Unfortunately celebrations of the Stormers' victory (with the customary stamping on posters of Reds players and shooting of AK-47s into the air) would have been cut short as news came in from Bangladesh that Biff Smith was blabbing about South Africa's thrashing by India. Smith, poor misguided child that he is, was reported as saying he got things a bit mixed up in arranging his bowling attack, and he had been guilty of a "tactical error" in not allowing Shaun Pollock to finish his full 10-over spell. If only Al-Sahaf had been on hand to explain the real situation ...

"There was no blunder. Brigadier Pollock bowled his full spell, and took 34 wickets in 11 deliveries, including three consecutive hat-tricks. Field Marshal Smith distinguished himself by scoring the first triple century in a one-day international."

Of course it will be a major setback to our sports if we don't get Comical Ali. Minister of Sports and Recreation Ngconde Balfour has shown flashes of promise with some solid doublespeak and workmanlike evasion, but so far his efforts have fallen short of the mark. Witness his reaction to the news that New Zealand football wallah Charles Dempsey would not be part of the World Cup 2010 bid-selection team, an all-too-frank "thank God" that the Kiwi was gone.

Ali would have had none of it. "We have never lost a bid. We win every bid we attempt. As for the New Zealand aggressor, here is footage of him taken in a Baghdad prison yesterday. Pay no attention to what seems to be the Waldorf Astoria behind him. The bid-rigging aggressor has been incinerated. His belly roasts in hell." **17.04**

Spooked by colour-coding

John Matshikiza

The huge picture on the front page of *The Star* said it all. There was Dubya, Master of the Universe, striding down a red carpet in the garden of the presidential guesthouse in Pretoria, with our own president trotting dutifully along beside him, trying to stay in the picture. Behind them, in soft focus, came the two first ladies. Even at that distance you could see Zanele Mbeki's mind trying to unravel how it was that she could have ended up, all these years later, trying to make polite conversation with Laura Bush in the pale winter sunshine of the highveld. "Ah, well," said the thought bubble above her head, clearly visible to the naked eye, "i-Job-i-job."

But study the picture closely. Don't forget that everything about

Darth Vader Jnr's visit to the Dark Continent had been planned to the last minute detail back in Washington DC. African airports had been closed and African airspace sealed off for the duration of the mercifully fleeting state visit. No chances were taken about anything.

So it was interesting to observe the colour-coding that had been specially organised for the presidents and their respective spouses. Both leaders were wearing boring navy blue suits, and their wives somewhat frumpish two-piece outfits. No Madiba shirts or loud, zappy, colourful Afro outfits here. But what a coincidence that the American president was wearing a bright red tie, to match his wife's bright red outfit, and that Thabo was wearing a blue one, matching his wife's suit.

One is left with the unavoidable conclusion that the CIA was taking no chances, and that strong colour-coding was the only way to ensure that Dubya would not end up holding hands with the wrong wife when it came time to take the official post-banquet photographs.

You think I'm joking? The same newspaper had carried another CIA-sponsored story just days before that had used equally large photographs of Mojanku Gumbi and Condoleeza (sic) Rice to illustrate not just the fact that both these darkie ladies were the most trusted and intimate advisers of their respective presidents, but that they also looked exactly the same, to boot!

One shall not digress into an interrogation of the subliminal racism that makes a respected honky journalist opine that all black women look alike. (I mean, for a start, our Mojanku has a much cuter nose, and certainly does not rejoice in those steely, "bring-me-the-head-of-John-the-Baptist-and-anyone-else-who-might-be-out-there" kind of Condoleezy eyes. But let's not get personal.)

The glaring fact is that clear colour-coding and large idiot cards held up in front of his face is the only way the richest nation on earth can keep its president looking on top of things. And you have to admire them for working like heck on this complex and difficult operation. I guess this is why the said Condoleezza was not also walking along that red carpet at the president's khaya, but had rather been relegated to the sidelines. No chances could be taken that, having got Dubya to hold hands with the right wife, he would then blow it all by going up to Condoleezza and saying, "Gee, thanks for a great lunch, Mrs Mbeki." It would have been hard to cover that one up — rather like trying to explain the absence of weapons of mass destruction in Iraq.

One is often inclined to feel increasing sympathy for the South African president's way of dealing with things, particularly when you hold him up shoulder-to-shoulder with his American counterpart. Take the war on terror, just for one example. America has gone out on a loud limb in its approach to this problem. Even while Dubya was on his state visit to South Africa, among other helpless countries on the continent, his government was imposing military sanctions on us for failing to toe the line on the issue of Americans' immunity from prosecution for war crimes, wherever and whenever they might have been committed — which was a strange and undemocratic position in itself. Yet while the US was bringing the message of anti-terrorist strategising to Africa, the whole world overlooked the fact that a terrorist threat of a different kind was being quietly dealt with by the South African government and its intelligence services.

The Boeremag is no joke. A large number of its members are currently on trial in Pretoria for plotting to overthrow the legitimately elected government of the country by force, justifying their antics with the claim that it was unconstitutional of the previous apartheid government to hand over the country to majority rule. The treason trial that these bonkers individuals are now being subjected to is being handled in a remarkably low-key fashion both by the government and the media.

One can only speculate that, from the government's side at least, the reason for this low-key treatment is to contain a potentially inflammatory and destabilising situation — particularly given that the Boeremag, loony-right fringe that it appears to be, might nevertheless represent a substantial body of racist opinion that is still skulking in the dark recesses of the South African psyche.

The reasons for the media's reticence are harder to fathom. But the impression one is left with is that, in tune with the thinking of the American government, terrorism is one thing when it comes in a brown skin, dressed in flowing Muslim robes and a long black beard, and quite another thing when it is perpetrated by the good-ol', pink-cheeked boys from the platteland in their khaki shorts, whose agenda is based purely on racial superiority on the African continent.

Did somebody say something about colour-coding? **18.07**

LETTER: IN BRIEF

John Matshikiza was back to Bush-whacking last week. Stupid Bush needs colour-coding to stop him mixing up Condoleezza Rice and Mrs Mbeki. Poor John needs gravitation-coding to stop him mixing up Boeremag bakkies and September 11 Boeings. — *Piet Erasmus, Kommetjie, 25.07*

Mbeki goes for the jugular

Drew Forrest

The late newspaper editor Ken Owen once described President Thabo Mbeki's political skills as "pathetic". He could not have been more wrong. Mbeki has outstanding gifts for instilling sheep-like obeisance in his party and neutralising and cutting down to size perceived or real opponents. As a political street-fighter whose business is winning, holding and building power, he is formidable.

In Parliament this week he showed why his sway over the African National Congress remains unchallenged despite the many mistakes he has made in his four years at the top. One could have heard an order paper drop during his quiet, disdainful, slightly unctuous reply to the State of the Nation debate, delivered in the manner of a headmaster at school assembly.

Earlier in the debate the hubbub of gossiping back-benchers had almost drowned out some MPs, forcing the Speaker to step in. Strong-minded men and women such as Sankie Mthembi-Mahanyele, Johnny de Lange, Derek Hanekom and Kader Asmal visibly basked in his approval. At his sarcastic shafts at the opposition, the ANC benches exploded in compliant guffaws.

Mbeki is a fearsome debater, expert at harnessing selected facts to his case, brushing aside opponents without engaging them and reversing moral onus on to his accusers. He also has an instinct for the jugular.

The universal complaint that his State of the Nation address had all but elided the pressing national issues of HIV/Aids and Zimbabwe was "puzzling", he said. The only possible solution to this "mystery" was that some had not read the speech. The "beating of the drums", he suspected, stemmed from differences with the policies of the government "rather than an economy of words on our part". One might have thought half his speech had been devoted to these two pressing national issues instead of the lone paragraph devoted to each.

And, lest anyone mistake his terseness on Aids for contrition about past error, he slipped in a defiant line about "the entire spectrum of diseases of poverty and underdevelopment, including those associated with immune deficiency".

The deft use of pointed silence to diminish criticism and redefine the agenda was clearest on the issue of state corruption, highlighted by both United Democratic Movement leader Bantu Holomisa and Democratic Alliance MP Raenette Taljaard. Taljaard made (and was forced to retract) a remark that the presidential entourage at the opening of Parliament resembled "an identification parade at a criminal investigation".

With ANC MP Tony Yengeni's fraud conviction hanging like a pall over the assembly, and Yengeni still sitting in the House, Taljaard and Holomisa presented a consolidated list of errant or accused servants of the state that included the national energy regulator, the former Civil Aviation Authority CEO, the former Spoornet CEO, a former public enterprises director, the public enterprises director general, the former Armscor chairperson, the former Denel chairperson, the SA Express CEO, the deputy president and the former ministers of transport and defence. To Taljaard's charge of government "limp-wristedness", and her reminder that he had not kept his pledge about a "cooling-off" period before former ministers went into business, the president said not a word.

Mbeki's tactic on another exposed flank, joblessness and economic stagnation, was to turn the tables by panning the opposition parties' "market fundamentalism" and, by implication, the indiscipline of the extra-parliamentary left ("through focused and painstaking work over the past few years, we are now able ...").

The "tide has turned" theme of his State of the Nation speech was picked up to project the image of an economy rebuilt on a solid base and now straining for an assault on poverty. "We have the necessary policies and programmes further to deepen the process of the reconstruction and development of our country. We have the resources to accelerate this process. Improved capacity does exist within the public service ..."

Mbeki simply blanked out the official opposition, his bête noire, referring to it once in his speech as "the DP". But he was at his deadliest in dealing with his Cabinet colleague and Inkatha Freedom Party leader Mangosuthu Buthelezi, whom he left smirking foolishly into the television cameras.

In his speech Buthelezi made the mistake of exposing his deepest longings for the respect and recognition of the ANC's top dogs. "We need to come together as people of goodwill ... I am deeply convinced that collegially we can exercise ... leadership," he pleaded. "We need to have a greater measure of respect for one another ... I somehow feel the suspicions of the past among ourselves have not vanished."

Given the rapprochement between the IFP and the DA, Mbeki was not about to give Buthelezi satisfaction. However "commendable" his call, none of the parties in Parliament, including the IFP, would relax their efforts to win power, he noted. IFP-DA cooperation in a bid for power was perfectly natural and normal political behaviour, Mbeki purred. But it had "nothing to do with the gathering of people of goodwill, of which the Honourable Dr Buthelezi spoke".
21.02

For whom has the tide turned?

Itumeleng Mahabane

We have turned the tide. Already the phrase slips easily off the tongues of journalists, analysts and party apparatchiks. One tries to imagine how the phrase forms itself in the dry, weary mouths of the unemployed millions. Perhaps for them it is pregnant with possibilities. Or perhaps it simply baffles them. It could be that they look about them incredulously, searching for the blinding neon of "wanted" signs that signify an economy turning the corner. The tens of thousands being retrenched probably spit the phrase out the way you might something that is off or venomous. Yet, we have turned that tide. So we are told.

None of the people expressing this sentiment — neither the president, who told us this, nor the corporate economists, who enthusiastically agree — offer any positive projections on the economy's ability to create jobs. They nod their heads in appreciation of the wonderful legacy of fiscal prudence and the glorious future of a slightly expansionary policy — nothing too brave, you understand.

Though no one suggests that the policies we have in place are even remotely capable of achieving growth of between 6% and 9% — levels we need if we are to fight unemployment — the tide has turned. Though we sit on a mountain of long-term savings and billions in deferred investment, even as the level of domestic investment remains insufficient to achieve the kind of growth that has a social impact.

This is not surprising. After all, for some, the South Africa economy is not in recession. For some, the performance of the economy in the past three or four years may not have been ideal, but it has been acceptable. The fortunate elite have been rewarded handsomely, not only through the joys of inflation-adjusted wage increases and bonuses, but through the more than R50-billion in tax cuts. For some the country has been growing steadily, while others have been living in a recession that has turned into a depression.

Joseph Stiglitz, the former chief economist of the World Bank who for more than six years has been rewriting the assumptions of the market fundamentalists, once wrote: "The most important policy for socially equitable development is full employment. The unemployed are not just a statistic or an under-utilised resource that could have increased gross domestic product [GDP]. They are people, and no numbers can convey the degree of disruption that unemployment brings to their lives, their livelihoods and the well-being of their families.

"Although safety nets and targeted assistance may mitigate some of the consequences of unemployment, from an economic, political or psychological perspective, nothing is better than a job. Jobs are the means by which people participate in the productive economy and feel productive themselves. It is one of the most important sources of inclusion in the national economy."

Any first year economics student will tell you that GDP growth is not an absolute measurement of economic progress. In fact, it is more useful for those economies closer to full employment. On its own, GDP growth is virtually useless for measuring progress in developing economies experiencing structural unemployment. This is for two reasons — both of which are applicable to South Africa. Firstly, GDP growth is rarely equitably distributed, unless there are clear government policy initiatives to ensure this. So you might achieve economic growth as well as a more rapid increase in inequality and poverty. Secondly, GPD growth may not correct economic decline, but simply prevent further recession.

Yet it has become commonplace in South Africa to measure our economic progress by comparing the GDP growth to that of developed countries. The private sector does this because ours is a country of two economies — one developed and one developing — and much of this sector has made it clear that it does not consider the developing economy a future market. The government does this because it cannot admit that the level of economic performance, coupled with unemployment and the legacy of woefully inadequate human capital, means adopting a much more creative economic policy.

Policy-makers in South Africa refuses to acknowledge that the majority live in an economic depression. One policy failure is the refusal to entertain the idea of a basic income grant. When the issue of a basic grant is raised, we are told the poor must enjoy the dignity of work and not handouts. Yet, Stiglitz argues, "spending money on social programmes can be complementary to the macroeconomic and structural policies discussed above. In the crudest terms, expanded social spending can be a very effective way to engineer a fiscal expansion."

For example, if a fiscal expansion is spent on physical infrastructure, then much of the money will be used to buy imports of capital equipment, blunting its expansionary consequences. Spending on social programmes keeps almost all of the money in the country, potentially leading to a larger output "multiplier".

This is not to say one should not invest in infrastructure. The Stiglitz argument suggests that in a country where unemployment is endemic and structural, social safety nets can have a positive effect on the economy. Assuming a basic multiplier, the grant proposal would result in a minimum R45-billion injection into the economy. Certainly, there can be little argument that the grant would not have the same positive effect on the economy as tax cuts.

There are other policy failures that suggest a disturbing inability to accept the fundamental reality of our economic state.

The promised micro-reforms outlined in last year's State of the Nation address have yet to come to fruition. The Department of Trade and Industry was supposed to deliver an industrial strategy, but came up with a shaky export strategy policy that virtually admitted it could not deal with unemployment. It failed the test of Parliament and we have heard little since.

The department's integrated manufacturing strategy was hardly ideal for job creation, but it is more disturbing that it has taken this long to return the document to Parliament — it was tabled in May. Given the deep structural deficiencies of the economy, including productivity, unemployment and poor levels of domestic investment, one would have thought that there is more urgency for micro-reform.

Similarly, the department's response to a broad-based, developmental empowerment policy has been pathetically slow in the making. When it came, it said nothing. Yet micro-reforms are the kinds of policy interventions that could have a lasting material effect on the majority of people.

The challenge is for a less rigid fiscal policy and a truly ambitious micro-economic policy. This is uncomfortable for many in the private sector and a few in the public sector to accept as they believe the government has no business in micro-economic reform; we cling to the Washington consensus that limits the government to fiscal and monetary policy. Having adopted the idea of market efficiency and market fundamentalism, our government is afraid of policies that are thought to be interventionist and might scare away investors. Stiglitz has shown how during the East Asian crises the International Monetary Fund forced those economies to enact policies that traded economic strength for investor confidence. It is now widely accepted that the institution's policy reforms exacerbated the crises.

The tide may indeed have turned, but for whom? **28.02**

Itumeleng Mahabane is a freelance journalist, working on a book on the history of black business

Case bares SA's racial bones

Fikile-Ntsikelelo Moya

In the movie *Mr Bones*, the lead character, a white guy who for some reason ends up as the chief traditional healer for some black tribe, gave some insight into our fascination with race, particularly regarding white kids who are raised in black communities.

Towards the end of the film, Mr Bones, the white sangoma, is called on to help a black woman in labour. He helps bring a bouncing white baby boy to Earth, much to the amazement of the locals, who had assumed that the chief was the child's father. The sangoma explains that he slept with the chief's wife because the chief was too ill to do so. The community accepts his explanation and its members get on with their lives.

Not so for Happy Sindane, the teenager who claims he was abducted from his white family by a black woman many years ago. There is widespread belief that were Happy a black street child who had emerged from rural homelands to search for his true parents there would not have been the same public interest or media attention. So why the fascination?

For some South Africans the events surrounding Happy's life bear the hallmark of the Tarzan story, but with the additional dimension of race. Happy's drama erupted when the fair-haired "white" boy walked into Bronkhorstpruit police station and declared, in fluent Ndebele, that he had been kidnapped from his white home by a black domestic worker 12 years earlier.

The police have found no evidence of Happy's proclaimed abduction. Instead, the statements gathered over the course of the investigation have convinced them that the domestic worker, who Happy referred to as Rina, was most probably his mother. The police findings, however, do not spell the end of Happy's story. Since his emergence from a rural backwater into urban society the media have leapt at various angles of the story and the police appear to have invested an uncharacteristic amount of resources in their effort to track down the boy's "real" family. They even wanted to cross the borders in an effort to find his father. This in a country where thousands of children grow up without knowing their real parents. So what was driving the South African Police Service to carry out such an unprecedented search?

According to police spokesperson Superintendent Morne van Wyk the police's role in the search for Happy's biological parents has now ended with the magistrate's conclusion that "on the balance of probabilities" the late Rina Mziyaya was his mother. Van Wyk said the case was now solely in the hands of the Gauteng department of social services and population development which could continue the search for Sindane's father if it wanted to.

Department spokesperson Panyaza Lesufi denied that government agencies had prioritised Happy's case above those of other children in similar situations. He said all 6 000 children under the department's care were given the same treatment. "It is the media that has treated this as a special case. But I don't blame them because it challenges the race relations issues and, as we all know, South Africa's history is characterised by race," said Lesufi. He said that Happy would remain in a place of safety until his case was finalised and he was returned to his family. The case resumes on August 19.

Dr Chris van Vuuren, a social anthropologist at the University of South Africa, believes the attention that Happy's story has received is indicative of the South African social situation. More particularly that of the white community, which, he said, is caught up in a Tarzan-like fascination with white children being raised by families of another race. "There have been numerous Hollywood movies made about tribal Indians raising white children in the Amazon jungle. Deep down in the minds of white people, especially, there is a perception that it is strange or abnormal that a child from a so-called civilised society could be raised in darkest Africa or the Amazon.

"In the South African case, apartheid made us believe that it is inconceivable that a white boy could be raised by black people. They ask themselves what type of morals and values he will have. What they forget is that the kid will grow up just like any other [child] in that community," said Van Vuuren.

Media specialist Graeme Addison said Happy's case was a "very South African story", but would probably not have received as much attention had Happy been a black boy. Addison said the attention given to Happy's story could be positive if it manages to highlight the problems of child neglect and abduction. "The media will always see a good human interest story. Provided they turn it into a social issue, I'm all for it. It should be the media's social responsibility to realise that this is one in hundreds of thousands of cases and then ask what is to be done. The issue should be a syringe to inject a new awareness. It needs to be a political issue. Child kidnapping and abduction for muti needs to be a major issue used to tick the consciences of politicians. There is no distinction between a black and a white kid but a white kid tends to be 10 times more newsworthy than a black one," said Addison.

For older South Africans Happy's story might be reminiscent of the "shame" brought on the Free State town of Excelsior in 1971. The international media descended on the dorpie, about 100km northeast of Bloemfontein, after the discovery that the town fathers, many of whom were leading lights in the National Party, had been running a sex ring involving their black domestic workers. Some of the disgraced men committed suicide rather than face charges under the Immorality Act, which criminalised inter-racial romances or liaisons.

Bond SA's Professor Jennifer Wilkinson, co-author of *Sexual Harassment in the Workplace,* believes that if Happy's case is one where an employer took advantage of his mother the story deserves the space it received. "What this has done is to throw issues such as maintenance, married men impregnating women and then denying it and the shame and psychological effects attached to this problem into the spotlight," Wilkinson said.

Addison believes Happy's story "needs to be dramatised". If this happens it could very well turn out to be a winning formula in the league of *Mr Bones*. Leon Schuster's film grossed R32-million locally before appearing at cinemas across Spain and Germany. **18.07**

Several hairstyles later, Happy Sindane was determined by the Bronkhorstspruit Magistrate's Court, in October 2003, to be Abbey Mzayiya, son of Rina Mzayiya. He was born in 1984. His "probable father", said the court, was Rina's then employer, Henry Nick. She abandoned Happy/Abbey in 1990 with Betty Sindane, who possibly misheard or mispronounced his name as "Happy".

Still no Happy ending

John Matshikiza

What the heck kind of a name is "Henry Nick" anyway? The young white prince found wandering in the forests of Mpumalanga, who turned out to be neither young, white nor, in fact, a prince, claims that he has finally discovered the true story of his heritage. Formerly known in the South African press as "Happy Sindane", it now turns out that his true name is Abbey Mzayiya. To their abiding shame, the newspapers got it all wrong from beginning to end.

Unfortunately for Abbey/Happy, this might not yet be the end of the road. His mother has been identified as the late Rina Mzayiya, and so he has now chosen to take her surname as his own, dropping that of his adoptive mother Betty Sindane. So far so good.

But it has now been revealed that his father was "probably" a shady German character who hung out on a smallholding at Fourways, just outside Johannesburg. The only record the police will admit to is that this German father (and Abbey's mother was probably neither the first nor the last black woman in the neighbourhood who received his attentions) rejoiced in the name of "Henry Nick". Which is why I ask the question: What the heck kind of a name is "Henry Nick" anyway?

I am worried that Happy/Abbey's tribulations are far from over, if this is all he knows about the man who fathered him in a moment of illicit passion with his part-time cleaning lady. Furthermore, Happy/Abbey now says that he "will try my best to find my father, if he is still alive". Where will he start? The Johannesburg telephone directory lists a "Nick Flooring", "Nick Transport Services" and "Nick's Fishmongers", but nobody who admits to the surname of "Nick". Most of these "Nicks" would probably turn out to be south Johannesburg merchants of Greek origin anyway, and the man our intrepid Happy/Abbey is looking for is supposed to be a German.

The way things work in this bitter racial space called South Africa, one can surmise that the gentleman in question probably told the unfortunate Rina Mzayiya that his name was Henry, but she could call him "Nick" for short. Being nothing more than a black woman, and a housemaid to boot, she would have assumed that she had to call him "Mr Nick", even during moments of intimacy. Thus "Nick" stuck in the minds of the locals as the man's proper surname, whereas it was probably nothing of the sort.

The police, of course, are too busy to care about details like this. As far as they are concerned, the case is closed. They would far rather be busying themselves with making sure that their car hijacking syndicates and little bits of this and that involving drugs and prostitution on the side are functioning smoothly and efficiently. Who can blame them? This Abbey has been an unhappy headache of paperwork, overtime sleuthing and unexpected moral dilemmas for several months now. Enough is enough.

The white press (replete with its complacent, newly appointed black editors in their wide and noisy BMWs) is also about to drop Happy/Abbey for the hot, brown potato that he has turned out to be. Now that there is no fairytale ending to look forward to, with the possibility of Happy/Abbey as a lost white prince finding a white princess anxiously waiting for him somewhere in Randfontein or Krugersdorp who couldn't sleep on a township bed if there was so much as one pea underneath the mattress, Happy/Abbey is rapidly becoming a non-story. So it behoves the few of us who have always been truly concerned about his future as an ordinary human being, regardless of race or gender, to pursue the Happy saga to the bitter end.

Happy should be so lucky. How many black, brown or indeterminate children are there out there whose German, Swiss, Russian or pukka British fathers have refused to acknowledge them (not to mention the legions of irresponsible darkies)? At least the paint company Dulux has admitted some responsibility and has allegedly established a trust fund worth R100 000 to support him for the next few years. Elsewhere it has been reported that he has a future as a radio disc jockey, simply by virtue of being himself.

Not since Monica "Splash-my-dress-so-I-can-kiss-and-tell" Lewinsky has fame and fortune come so quickly and easily. But unlike Lewinsky, it seems unlikely that Happy/Abbey will actually get his own TV chat show on prime-time television, even in South Africa. (And prime-time television is where the real money lies.) To begin with, Happy/Abbey's command of pseudo-American-English, so desirable for black prime-time chat show hosts in South Africa, is far from being up to scratch. So radio it will have to be (if that).

But things could be worse. There is a top-notch public relations company that is looking after all the details of just exactly what Abbey is going to need to remain Happy for the foreseeable future.

Yes, things could be much worse. We recall, for example, that Happy/Abbey's sad entry into the world began when his mother's common-law husband, one Thomas Banda, refused to accept him into the household because he was the son of a white chap, and told his mother to send him away into the wilderness — rather like a certain young man who was abandoned by his own mother, only to be found by Pharoah's daughter and given the name of Moses.

Imagine — if the unpleasant stepfather had accepted Abbey/Happy into the homestead, he might have had to be content to go through life being known as plain old Abbey Banda, with no prospects whatsoever. As it is, he might yet go on to lead us all into the Promised Land. Every cloud, however black it might seem to those who are gazing up from the ground, does, after all, have a silver lining. There might yet be a Happy ending after all. **03.10**

Just another dorpie

Rapule Tabane

The Vierkleur and the old Boer Republic flags no longer adorn the streets of Ventersdorp. The terrifying sight of Afrikaner Weerstandsbeweging leader Eugene Terreblanche and his masked Ystergaard warriors is no more. Also missing are regular reports of lynching of blacks in this town.

The town has become like any other South African dorp. But change is more than the absence of terror or of naked racism, as its citizens are finding out. Now, under African National Congress local government on a council with eight ruling party councillors and two from the Democratic Alliance, one would expect a transformed town with delivery on the boil.

Not so for the people of Tshing township and the surrounding rural areas. Take Dora Schalkwyk. This week she went to the Ventersdorp police station to lay a charge against "my own government". Schalkwyk had reached the end of her tether because she felt local government officials were denying her and other women the opportunity to earn a living.

Schalkwyk runs an empowerment project with four other women sewing tracksuits and other garments for local schoolchildren, but the project is now high and dry. The local economic development project had over two years trained many women who went on to open their own dressmaking businesses. Part of their profits was handed over to the council to assist in community development. Schalkwyk claims they have been handing over their earnings to the local municipality for the past two years.

But a month ago the council disconnected the water and electricity from their premises. Tracksuit production stopped and cabbages in adjacent vegetable projects started wilting. It did not end there. Officials from the municipality allegedly jumped through the windows of the locked offices and removed some computer equipment and documents. That was when Schalkwyk decided to take the legal route.

The question is: why would a local municipality take such action when the project is typical of both the food security and public works programmes discussed in the Cabinet's *lekgotla*? The municipality says the project owes money for water and electricity for the premises and its members are unwilling to share their facilities with other people. Community members, however, say the answer lies in the Ventersdorp council's failure "to use its power effectively" and in the fact that a white-dominated administration is running the show. Residents allege that while Ventersdorp has slain its biggest racial dragons, transformation has not seeped down to its grassroots.

Municipal manager Zaid Bhabha confirms that of his top four managers two are black and two white and that the rest of middle management is white. But he denies that this has an impact on delivery. "Obviously we have an affirmative action policy but it can't just throw people out of jobs," Bhabha contended.

While driving around Tshing township, with its many old and dilapidated houses, we discovered a group of youngsters jumping through a gap in the wall to the old Tshing community hall where they practise dancing and singing in preparation for regional competitions. The municipality has locked the hall and intends selling it off. Local playwright Velaphi Kaqankase says: "They deny us access to the hall and expect us to pay, irrespective of whether it is just a rehearsal or a live performance. As emerging artists we find that problematic as we are trying to stay off the streets."

The alternative is a new hall where they are expected to pay R250 a year and an unspecified amount every time they use it, an example of the cost recovery programmes that many municipalities institute because they are cash-strapped.

North-West provincial local government MEC Darkie Afrika insists that youth cannot be expected to pay for a service if they do not make a profit from it, but the council still insists on payment. "That was a decision taken by a white manager who does not understand the township culture. How can you charge youth instead of encouraging efforts to get them off street corners and shebeens?" asks Lawrence Motlhoiwa of the Ventersdorp Community Development Forum

Not far from the locked hall is a recently opened bottle store that was a council beer hall before the building was closed and sold off to a businessman. Besides the fact that the bottle store is next to a school, Kaqankase complains that the youth had expected the council to keep the building for recreational use. Bhabha says the buyer of the premises never indicated that he would open a liquor outlet and that only the provincial administration had the authority to deal with liquor licence applications.

An estimated 70% of Ventersdorp's citizens are unemployed — the biggest challenge facing the government. The town is situated in what used to be the Western Transvaal and the economy is heavily reliant on agriculture and a handful of industries. In the past two years the biggest investment in the town has been the establishment of an OK supermarket. Other than that, Bhabha says, there are some basic micro-economic development projects.

Ventersdorp's integrated development plan aims to reduce unemployment by 25% by 2006 by establishing at least 10 emerging farmers a year and marketing the area and its products. Bhabha says the council is committed to ensuring that every council project is labour intensive. The council is currently trying to raise R12-million to repair its potholed roads to create jobs and develop infrastructure. But so far only R2-million has been made available by the North West government, Bhabha says. He adds that plans to build up to 2 000 new low-cost houses have just been finalised.

The council claims that it provides free basic water, although residents deny the claims. Council administrator Jaco van der Merwe said the council does not have the resources to provide free electricity. For poverty-stricken residents who cannot afford to pay their rates, the council has an indigent policy, but resident Cornelius Mokgethi claims that this serves a disproportionate number of white residents because most township residents are unaware that such a policy exists.

For residents who owe the council money there is no recourse. Bhabha explains the council's "60-40" policy of debt management where a resident buys R10 worth of electricity, but only receives R4 worth with the R6 channeled into his/her arrears. The average rate of payment for services is 50%. "There is no economic development and I want to ask this council: 'In five years where do they see service delivery improving and economic development happening?' The problem is that when you ask too many questions you are labelled a political opponent," says Mokgethi, who also complains that there are no ward committees in operation and therefore no platform for residents to air their views on governance.

Meanwhile, Schalkwyk is inconsolable: "When we elected these people they promised to look after us and to eradicate poverty but they destroy a poverty eradication project! The other three women have given up and only two of us are left to battle the council. This place breaks my heart." **25.07**

"**Falling asleep is unintentional.**" — Jeanette Vilakazi, an Inkatha Freedom Party MP, after parliamentarians called for television stations to stop photographing them sleeping through debates. 22.08

Another Dullah Omar brain-child pregnancy goes pop

Robert Kirby

With about 100m to go before the R43 reaches the town of Worcester in the Western Cape, there used to stand on either side of the road two of those large Arrive Alive signboards. I'm sure you know the kind, mounted alongside roads, exhibiting motor vehicle statistics, the percentage of vehicles recorded speeding, the number of accidents. Presumably these figures related to the stretch of road where each signboard stood.

When dreaming up this signboard campaign did the Minister of Transport, Dullah Omar, and his advisers seriously consider practical realities? Did they believe that, seeing one of these signboards, the average motorist would actually pull up, reverse along the side of the road and take time out to read and absorb the statistics displayed? There was far too much information on the signboards to be read by a driver travelling even slowly, and whose attention, anyway, would be distracted from the more important business of driving safely.

The signboards were another genetically unstable brainchild of Dullah Omar's department and, like others before it, is now in the process of being aborted. In the Department of Transport's "Strategies Nursery" there's not a lot of difference between the infants and the infantile.

South African motorists will no longer be required to read and be deeply "incentivised" — to use one of Dullah's stylish coinages — to drive responsibly by Arrive Alive signboards. They are currently being scrapped, thrown away, dispatched for burial. I don't have figures for the rest of the country, but the Western Cape had 220 of the signboards, so it may be assumed that the national total could be well in excess of a thousand, maybe two.

How many millions of public money were squandered on this enterprise? How many hundreds of thousands of precious traffic police man-hours were wasted on the updating of the statistics, sometimes to ludicrous effect. The two signboards outside Worcester stood opposite each other and regularly displayed totally conflicting figures. And should you think the signboards futile, you should listen to the excuses for the road carnage that have emanated from the Department of Transport while Dullah's been steering.

Bless his tasteful *djellabahs*, Dullah Omar has never publicly been known to concur with any opinion that shows even a hint of conflicting with his own. Questioned about the road massacres of the recent holiday season, Omar fell back on the conventional ministerial response to difficult questions: first he blamed the road fatalities on "our past" and then assured dolefully that "future strategies" are being "worked on" — thereby cannily dispatching his obligations safely out of the present. "Anyone who has a better idea is welcome to get in touch with us," blathered Omar, jiggling his eye-bags, implying that an indifferent public was to blame for inadequacies in government policy.

Minister Omar's professional relationship with Trevor Abrahams, suspended CEO of the Civil Aviation Authority, has now come under brighter lights. The allegations against Abrahams are profoundly disturbing and one can't help but wonder what will be Dullah Omar's response if these allegations are proved to have foundation. Some of the chicanery of which Trevor Abrahams now stands accused would appear to have taken place right under Omar's nose. It was Omar who reinstated Abrahams after an earlier scandal was quietly settled at departmental level. If this reinstatement is ever proved to have been an ill-considered decision, will Dullah Omar have to own up to his responsibility?

Any government minister possessed of but a smidgeon of self-doubt would have resigned faced with the sort of appalling road-death tragedy that faces Dullah Omar. He shouldn't even have to wait for the loud demands for resignation. They only made him haughtier. "I'm 68," he fumed, "and I've never resigned from anything in my life."

More's the pity. The "new" South Africa has had to endure Dullah Omar in other than his current role. As it painfully recovers from its past, the justice department owes little to the Omar suzerainty. Admittedly there were highlights: he did drive out to the airport to embrace the African National Congress's pet funds-hustler, Allan Boesak.

The Mbeki administration has this quaint need both to accommodate and succour overbearing political turkeys. Taking their lead from the boss, there exists a cabal of decidedly sub-standard ministers and senior executives in current government structures whose reaction to criticism of their often hideous ineptitude is usually a blend of hostility and arrogance. Our minister of health is an embarrassing case in point.

There's little profit to joining the indignant throng of those demanding minsterial and other resignations, simply because such demands always seem to have the reverse effect on our state president. Calling for the resignation of an Mbeki appointee is a virtual guarantee of that individual's continued occupation of his or her position — if not promotion. The suspended ANC chief whip, Tony Yengeni, faces serious criminal charges of corruption and lying. Mr Mbeki has now charged him with the investigation of corruption in the Eastern Cape administration. Perhaps that's how Thabo Mbeki wants to be remembered, as the man who both selected and nurtured some truly abject incompetents. **17.01**

Looking for an MP in a haystack

Marianne Merten

In the search for MPs in about 20 parliamentary constituency offices this week, we had just one close encounter, missed by a mere 10 minutes: MPs had either "just left" or were at the office only on certain days. Several were elsewhere in the country, or at Parliament (which was closed).

Constituency work was officially set down from April 22 to May 9. But at every office there was at least one administrator, each with the required computers, phones and fax machine at hand. Decorating tastes ranged from the discreet yellow, black and green blinds at the African National Congress's Mitchells Plain office to those who had turned their offices into party megaphones.

At the New National Party's Mitchells Plain office, wallpaper posters of leader Marthinus van Schalkwyk across the vast office left little doubt where you were. The NNP offices face a conundrum dictated by the party's quicksand-like allegiances. Now split from the Democratic Alliance, its offices are still listed under the DA name in the telephone directory. But each office has posters on issues like human rights and at least one on Parliament. There are usually stacks of government information pamphlets on, for example, the Unemployment Insurance Fund.

At the ANC's Mitchells Plain office several women waited for assistance. It is the office of Minister of Finance Trevor Manuel, whose Cabinet duties prevent him from making frequent visits, and former trade union leader Connie September, who is on study leave.

In the DA's Kenilworth office, shared by MPs Dene Smuts and Ken Andrew, party leader Tony Leon was staring from election posters at the abandoned desks. Even the administrator had gone out to help contest Wednesday's by-election in Grassy Park on the Cape Flats.

In the absence of accessible government, the constituency offices double as public office and advice centres. On a daily basis administrators deal with a string of queries. Sometimes people want to pay TV licences or water bills. Some are at their wits end over bureaucratic snarl-ups with social grants and identity documents. Others face evictions and water or electricity cut-offs or banks wanting to repossess their cars.

It's easy to spot the Grassy Park ANC constituency office on the first floor of another little neighbourhood "shopping centre" — the party emblem and "ANC parliamentary constituency office" are painted on one of the windows facing the street. "Imam [Gassan Solomon] has just left," said administrator Nolene Blows. Faced with people who come to the office with their problems, Blows works with well-established networks to help resolve problems.

While a random telephone survey found only one MP actually answering his office phone, cellphone numbers and other details were promptly supplied. "Comrade [Derek] Hanekom? He is on his way to Johannesburg. You can reach him on his cell," said the Kimberley ANC constituency office, giving the number.

Eleven weeks are set aside for constituency work between February's opening of Parliament and its close of session in mid-December. Apart from lawmaking, being avaliable to constituencies is key to MPs' work, for which they are paid a R5 000 monthly allowance to run their offices. Each of South Africa's 400 parliamentarians, selected from party lists on the basis of the votes each party scores in elections, is allocated to a constituency.

This year the Cabinet decided to keep this system for next year, rejecting a recommendation by the Electoral Task Team that a substantial number of MPs should be elected through 69 constituencies. The constituency system is not a well-oiled machine, if a recent Afrobarometer poll is anything to go by. It found that only one in 10 South Africans knew who their MP was. MPs might have been difficult to track down in their constituency offices, but this does not mean they were goofing off. The staff of the ANC's Grassy Park and Guguletu offices listed the MPs' meetings with police, local community policing forums and other local civic groups during the constituency period.

At the Guguletu ANC office two young girls sat in the sun. They are part of the learnership programme the office runs for about 100 matrics who cannot afford further studies. "You have just missed the MP. She was here 10 minutes ago," said administrator Xoliswa Ngubane.

Constituency work should filter back to Parliament as questions or statements by members and on committee agendas, but does it? In Parliament, it often does not seem that way as debates are often esoteric with research culled from newspapers rather than grassroots based. Party chief whips say they are keeping track: the ANC through quarterly reports, the DA through yearly performance assessments. DA chief whip Douglas Gibson said that, in addition to a code of conduct, MPs are specifically asked to visit schools, clinics or police stations. "If you like politics and people, the constituency period is a wonderful experience," he said.

The ANC has adopted a more activist approach, with MPs getting involved in community affairs and individual problems. "We don't want them to go there to sit in an office behind the desk," said ANC chief whip Nkosinathi Nhleko.

So, how precisely do you get hold of your MP? Getting in touch with constituency offices can be tough. In King William's Town in the Eastern Cape calls to the ANC constituency telephone numbers listed in Parliament's guide were met with: "The number you have dialled is presently not in service." A call to the provincial ANC head office led to another telephone number and another out-of-order number, an expensive and frustrating task if you're a poor constituent. Without Internet and phone access, it's almost impossible.

So, for South African voters trying to get in touch with their MPs, it could be a case of not-so-close encounters. But 2004 is an election year, so things might just look up. **9.05**

In search of a new moral DNA

Mondli Makhanya

We all remember the image: Winnie Madikizela-Mandela arriving in Soweto after defying her banishment to arid Brandfort. Fist in the air, defiant smile on her face and hundreds of supporters crowded around her four-roomed house, she was the picture of the self-confidence that the anti-apartheid struggle was about.

She was then an unblemished icon — the face of the revolution being fought in the streets of South Africa. She was the personification of her imprisoned husband and the voice of Oliver Tambo and the exiled leadership, whose words apartheid's repressive laws would not let us hear. Hers, then, was a struggle about morality, about the decent society that was being sought and about the high ideals that the liberation movements were preaching.

So when Madikizela-Mandela was convicted of fraud and theft last week, it was that decency and those high ideals that she was found guilty of betraying. It was not a moment to be celebrated, even by those who detest Madikizela-Mandela. It was a sad moment. It was also a moment that should cajole us into examining how one in whom the nation had invested so much faith turned against the ideals for which she fought. By extension it should prompt within us a deep introspection about how so many who gave up so much in order that a good society be created have become the parasites.

History is replete with examples of revolutions that went wrong, liberation movements that turned against the people and heroic figures who became villains. Recent events have enabled us to realise how things can go very wrong if heroes are not kept on their toes. What these events reveal is the need for introspection that will prevent us from handing to future generations a rotten republic in which morality is blurred.

The conviction of Tony Yengeni and Madikizela-Mandela prove to us that the post-liberation struggle is the more difficult one and one in which the foe is not easily identifiable. And the destruction of Zimbabwe (once a model for the management of post-liberation societies) by those who liberated the country shows that liberation-era ideals are assets to be treasured and protected even if they appear unfashionable.

The South African project is one in which an entire nation is seeking to rebuild itself, in which we are trying to redefine ourselves and refine our belief systems. At the centre of this national redefinition should be the key value of morality, the standard around which all debate about growth paths, empowerment, patriotism and national interest should pivot.

Morality was the ideal that was the antithesis of apartheid. But along the way we have got lost and seem to have adapted to the ideals-starved post-Cold War era. We take short cuts and when caught employ the lazy defences of racial and political party solidarity. Lazy racial solidarity surely explains why white South Africa reacts with righteous indignation to any suggestion that Hansie Cronje died an evil man.

Yet these self-same defenders of the crooked cricketer will jump at every opportunity to call for the heads of Yengeni and Madikizela-Mandela. Flip the race coin and you will find a stoic defence of struggle veterans who, like Cronje, received late-night calls from the devil. These "comrades" suffered immensely at the hands of the apartheid security forces, the crude defence will go. Their crookedness becomes some sort of post-apartheid stress syndrome.

And so it is argued that it's wrong for Allan Boesak, Yengeni and Madikizela-Mandela to suffer the consequences of their post-apartheid greed. Their defenders point to the fact that the FW de Klerks, Adriaan Vloks and Philip Powells are still walking free while struggle heroes are being tried for lesser crimes.

If ever there was a perverse sense of morality this is it. To use the Nats and the lieutenants of the tetchy chief from Ulundi as moral standards is to admit to being morally unambitious. Surely a higher level of morality is required of those leaders who should now be instrumental in the building of the new republic? The African National Congress, in particular, has a calling and responsibility way beyond its membership and support base. The majority of South Africans identify with the ANC not only as a political party but also as an instrument with which they form their opinions and value systems.

This is the nature of the relationship between liberated people and the movements that liberate them. Zimbabwe is rotten today because it allowed its primary liberation movement to be infected with greed and self-aggrandisement. As is the case with Angola, where one of the world's most sophisticated liberation movements was transformed into a gang of thieving parasites who forgot about why the struggles against Portuguese colonialism and later against Western imperialism were fought in the first place.

South Africa has a chance to avoid that fall and build on the morality that created the likes of Albert Luthuli, Yusuf Dadoo and Moses Kotane. That morality is still present among many who were brutalised by the apartheid regime. We can still learn from the likes of Albertina Sisulu, Ellen Khuzwayo and Sister Bernard Ncube.

They too suffered immensely but refuse to sink to their former oppressors' level of morality. It is from those like them that we should draw DNA as we define the character of our republic. **02.05**

LETTERS

ANC's conscience lies in the gutter

The ANC leadership is corrupt, and South Africans should not allow this situation to continue. Like Tony Yengeni, Winnie Mandikizela-Mandela, the president of the ANC Women's League, is accused of fraud. The ANC has lambasted the Inkatha Freedom Party-Democratic Alliance coalition, whereas the ANC is in coalition with that strong stakeholder of apartheid, the New National Party. It is time that we elected people of honour, who respect our money and can make South Africa governable. — *NA Sibiya, Louwsburg, 07.03*

ANC is milking the country dry

By the time the African National Congress is removed from office, it will have milked the country dry. From Winnie Madikizela-Mandela to Tony Yengeni, from Miles Nzama to Terror Lekota, from oil deals to arms deals, these ANC people are lining their pockets at the expense of the poor majority. The ANC has failed to deliver on the mandate given by poor, rural black people and has gone into cahoots with big business. White South Africans rave about the Rainbow Nation and the virtues of the New Partnership for Africa's Development, but many black South Africans have not discovered the pot of gold at the end of the rainbow. I'm definitely voting next year — against greed, corruption and non-delivery. The ANC won't get my vote. — *Thulani Shenge, Cape Town 06.06*

Oil scandal rocks SA

Stefaans Brümmer and Sam Sole

On August 26 1999 Phumzile Mlambo-Ngcuka, then still wet behind the ears as Minerals and Energy Minister, briefed journalists in Parliament: "South Africa is diversifying [its] sources of crude oil; and we are happy that Nigeria has made this allocation for us. Our officials in the Department of Minerals and Energy [and] the Department of Foreign Affairs will be looking at the modalities of transporting it."

Had the minister's statement not been so utterly misleading, it might have helped clear up the confusion sowed a week earlier when *Business Day* broke the news locally. President Olusegun Obasanjo's government, the business daily said, had allocated South Africa the right to lift, or market, 55 000 barrels of Nigerian crude a day; a government-to-government contract that was a first between the two countries. It also cited the surprise of an unnamed official who said South Africa "was not involved in tendering for the allocation". And it quoted Rod Crompton, the man who really should have known as he was Mlambo-Ngcuka's chief director of liquid fuels, as saying he had no knowledge of it. In the absence of official elaboration, the only sense that *Business Day* could make of the allocation was to call it an "unsolicited gift" that, according to industry representatives, "could constitute a statement by the Nigerian government aimed at improving relations with South Africa".

Mlambo-Ngcuka's address to the hacks in Parliament was misleading for a simple reason: it perpetuated the pretence that this oil allocation, the largesse bestowed by Nigeria, was to be handled by the government of South Africa for the benefit of the people of South Africa. In fact, Mlambo-Ngcuka's officials and their counterparts at foreign affairs were not to exercise their minds on "the modalities of transporting" the oil to South Africa. Neither the oil, nor the revenue, was to come to South Africa. Ruling party-aligned interests were lined up to benefit (although, as will be seen, some may not have). And the people of South Africa were certainly not to benefit.

Mlambo-Ngcuka's "mistake" may have been excusable as she was new to the job: only two months earlier had she been elevated to the minerals and energy portfolio in President Thabo Mbeki's first Cabinet. But she might have been better informed had she consulted with a number of colleagues in the government or comrades in the African National Congress.

For starters she may have asked her immediate predecessor in the portfolio, current Minister of Justice and Constitutional Development Penuell Maduna, to make some inquiries on her behalf. While Maduna this week denied involvement in securing the contract or having had knowledge of it at the time, a confidant of his, Brian Casey, was central to it. Casey, who acted as general manager of the state's Strategic Fuel Fund during Maduna's term as minerals and energy minister, was the first chief executive of the company originally lined up to scoop the deal. Maduna also confirmed to the *Mail & Guardian* that he knew Kase Lawal, the Nigerian-American businessman who was behind it all.

Mlambo-Ngcuka could also have turned for advice to Minister of Provincial and Local Government Sydney Mufamadi, whose wife, Nomusa Mufamadi, became a director of the company. Or to Eastern Cape Premier Makhenkesi Stofile, whose brother-in-law, Hintsa Siwisa, became chair. Or ANC treasurer general Mendi Msimang, whose sidekick and party fundraiser, Miles Nzama, became a director.

And then, Mlambo-Ngcuka could have sought clarification from Minister of Trade and Industry Alec Erwin, under whom Mlambo-Ngcuka had served as deputy minister until two months earlier and who only a month earlier had visited Nigeria. Or she could have asked President Thabo Mbeki, whose correspondence to Obasanjo, borne by Erwin on that trip, was instrumental in clinching the deal.

Another falsehood was being perpetuated at the time: Nigeria, then only six months into the civilian administration of Obasanjo, said it would cut the corruption that characterised its lifeblood oil industry. Under previous military dictatorships many crude lifting contracts had gone to cronies, at a substantial discount, who on-sold their allocations at market rates. They split the margin between themselves and their politico-military patrons.

Africa Confidential, under the headline "Cleaning up oil", explained: "Under previous governments, crude sales were a fountain of political patronage, as military officers and politicians sponsored traders' bids for contracts. Out of such deals the 'sponsor' could earn as much as five [US] cents a barrel, which added up nicely when some sponsors controlled more than 70 000 barrels a day ... The commission system may have cost the NNPC [the state oil company, the Nigerian National Petroleum Corporation] as much as $1,5-billion a year."

What Obasanjo's government and the NNPC did to "clean up" the oil industry in July 1999 was to cancel all 41 lifting contracts awarded by the former military regime and announce a "transparent" process to award new contracts. These new contracts, the state oil company said, would cut out the crony intermediaries. To qualify, bidders had to be "bona fide end-users" — that is, companies that owned their own refineries — or recognised "large volume traders". Qualifying bidders would also have to show commitment to Nigeria by investing in community development or the energy sector.

When the NNPC announced the successful candidates for the new one-year "term contracts", as they are called, in August 1999, 13 well-known refiners and traders were included. Three countries that would get "government-to-government" contracts — and it was widely reported as such — were also on the list: Kenya, Ghana and South Africa. In Kenya and Ghana's case the successful bidders were reportedly their national oil companies. In the remaining case the recipient was noted simply as "South Africa".

As it turned out the "South African" recipient would fall into none of the above categories: it was not an end-user; it was not a recognised large volume trader; it was not a government. Certainly, the state and the people of South Africa were not to benefit. The company that signed the contract was registered in the Cayman Islands, both a tax haven and a haven of corporate anonymity. Named the "South African Oil Company", it indeed had little to do with South Africa. It was part of Lawal's Camac Group, an oil-and-gas enterprise headquartered in the United States oil capital of Houston, Texas.

But let's go back in time. South Africa and Nigeria, the two economic powers of Africa, had been on bad terms for decades; the one a racist autocracy, the other a series of military dictatorships. When democracy came to South Africa in 1994 Nigeria lagged behind. Relations hit rock bottom the following year when General Sani Abacha's regime executed imprisoned democracy activist Ken Saro-Wiwa. Then-president Nelson Mandela, in his own words "almost out of control" with anger, spearheaded Nigeria's suspension from the Commonwealth.

That was all to change when, in February 1999, Obasanjo, himself formerly imprisoned by Abacha, was elected civilian president. Obasanjo was a man South Africa could do business with, so to speak. The foundation was laid for a strong relationship between two countries that would be pillars of the New Partnership for Africa's Development.

As seems to be the case in international relations, commerce followed politics. Between 1998 and 1999 two-way trade jumped from R730-million to R1,7-billion. South Africa had technological expertise to offer; hence, for example, the cellular phone network established in Nigeria by South African telecom group MTN and, more recently, fuel giant Sasol's involvement in a gas-to-liquid fuel plant there. Nigeria had its single dominant export to offer: crude oil.

While Maduna denies that, as outgoing minister, he had anything to do with the negotiations for the contract, Erwin and Mbeki did. Department of Foreign Affairs correspondence obtained by the *M&G* gives the first clue. On August 12 1999 South Africa's high commission in the Nigerian capital, Abuja, wrote to Obasanjo's special adviser on petroleum, Obasanjo's minister for cooperation in Africa and the managing director of the NNPC to brief them on a forthcoming visit to their country by "a high-level investment team" from the South African state oil and gas company Soekor (now part of PetroSA). The letter said: "You will no doubt be aware of the exchange of correspondence between President Obasanjo and President Mbeki on the term contract for oil sales between Nigeria and South Africa."

An attached briefing note elaborated: "The [Soekor] visit is in response to the recent correspondence relating to oil and gas sales and investment which was exchanged between President Mbeki and President Obasanjo. This correspondence was conveyed during the visit to Nigeria of Minister Alec Erwin, Minister of Trade and Industry, during July 1999." Soekor, the note said, was "specifically interested in providing funding and technical expertise to projects in Nigeria, especially within the field of oil production".

But why would a South African state company have been interested in investing in Nigeria "in response to" Mbeki's correspondence with Obasanjo on a term contract to lift Nigerian oil? It may have been coincidence that Soekor was heading to Nigeria exactly when South Africa was asking for the oil contract, but it appears also to have been convenient as it corresponded with one of the conditions set by the NNPC for qualifying bidders: "commitment" to Nigeria through investment in the energy sector.

And so, even though a Caymans-registered private company, the so-called South African Oil Company, was to benefit from the oil contract, South African state resources were expended on the contract. It was not the first time and, as will be seen, it seems not to have been the last. On August 16 — four days after the high commission's briefing note — the deal was on. The NNPC wrote a letter addressed simply to "the Republic of South Africa", care of the South African high commission, with the heading "Offer of One Year Crude Oil Contract".

The NNPC letter said: "We refer to your application on the above mentioned subject and wish to convey management's approval to offer a 55 000 barrels per day crude oil contract for one (1) year to you." The offer, clearly, was to the "Republic of South Africa". The NNPC letter also asked, pro forma, for details of the intended contracting party's corporate identity including its certificate of incorporation and its memorandum of association, the latter of which states the company's operational purpose. The fun was about to start.

Documents at the Registrar of Companies in Pretoria show that a South African-registered company, also connected to Lawal's Camac Group, was at first the intended beneficiary. This company had started its life in 1997 as Camac International Trading SA, with the main object "to carry on the business of a principal trading company in the mining industry of solid minerals".

This, of course, was not good enough for a company that wanted to scoop South Africa's lifting rights to Nigerian crude oil. Not only was "solid minerals" a problem, but Camac, due to its links with its US parent company, might have sounded decidedly un-South African. And so, on August 19 1999 — three days after the NNPC's request for company details — lawyers in Pretoria lodged an application, stamped "urgent", to the companies registrar. The application was to reserve the name "South African Oil Company" — the same name as Lawal's Cayman entity — with the main object "to carry on the business of trading and managing crude oil".

There was a momentary hiccup when the registrar disallowed that name on the grounds that it was too similar to that of an existing entity. But the registrar allowed the name "SAOC Oil Company", an awkward abbreviation of the same name that was being sought.

After another application in December, the registrar relented: Camac had transformed into the "South African Oil Company". This local namesake of Lawal's Cayman-registered company, while 49% owned by another two of Lawal's companies, included as shareholders and directors a number of ANC-aligned individuals and interests. The main players in this company were Hintsa Siwisa (chair, 11% shareholder, brother-in-law of Eastern Cape Premier Makhenkesi Stofile); Nomusa Mufamadi (executive director, 5% shareholder, wife of Provincial and Local Government Minister Sydney Mufamadi) and Brian Casey (chief executive, former acting general manager of the Strategic Fuel Fund, confidant of Minister Maduna).

These three, by all appearances, played a role not only in this local version, but also in the business of the South African Oil Company registered in the Caymans. Other planned shareholders or directors in the local company included entities related to two more relatives of Stofile; a company that in 1999 included Mathuding Ramathlodi, wife of Limpopo Premier Ngoako Ramathlodi; Women's Development Bank Investment Holdings (WDBIH), linked to First Lady Zanele Mbeki's WDB Trust; and Zwelibanzi "Miles" Nzama, the ANC fundraiser and dealmaker. Some of these, however, said they had either withdrawn or not received any shares. A 25% shareholding remained opaque because of incomplete registration.

On August 18, two days after the NNPC's letter to "the Republic of South Africa", the South African Oil Company, address Johannesburg, wrote to NNPC managing director Jackson Gaius-Obaseki "to thank NNPC for selecting us as one of the Nigerian crude oil lifters ... We applaud your leadership of NNPC for the transparency through which the exercise was conducted."

The letter continued, again emphasising government's — and specifically Mbeki's — involvement: "SAOC, through the support of the government of South Africa, will do everything to live up to the confidence of NNPC in us ... A copy of our application submitted through the office of the President of the Republic of South Africa and other related correspondents [sic] are attached for your records. We hope that SAOC will receive a copy of the letter of award together with NNPC draft contract as soon as possible."

The contract, however, was not signed by the South African entity. Lawal's Cayman-registered South African Oil Company stepped in to sign the deal with Nigeria. How did that change the beneficiary breakdown? While the South African-registered company was 49% owned by Lawal's Camac Group, the Cayman company is, according to the Camac Group website, 75% owned by it. The rest is not declared. Lawal this week refused to elaborate, saying it was "irrelevant". The directors and shareholders of Cayman offshore companies, as this is, are not publicly declared and are protected by secrecy laws.

In October 1999 the oil started flowing. A contemporaneous industry publication, citing an announcement by the Nigerian high commissioner to South Africa, said: "Nigeria started supplying 55 000 barrels per day of crude oil to South Africa." It also said: "Earlier, South African President Thabo Mbeki commended Nigeria's decision to allocate 55 000 barrels of crude oil to his country, stating that it marked the 'first great step at cooperation between the two greatest African nations.'"

The South African Oil Company, Cayman, was now the proud recipient of 55 000 barrels of Nigerian crude each day — enough to fill a large crude carrier every month or so. But were these crude carriers to set sail for South Africa? No. The South African Oil Company engaged Glencore, a Swiss-based international trading company, as its "risk management" partner. That means the allocation was on-sold to Glencore.

Glencore would have paid the South African Oil Company a fixed amount per barrel of crude, while Glencore took its chances selling the oil on the international market to see what extra margin it could make: the intermediary system revived and the purpose of the NNPC's "transparent" new contracts defeated. With little effort other than bagging a contract that had been secured with the assistance of the South African government, the private South African Oil Company, Cayman, was assured substantial and steady profits.

How much were those profits? Oil traders estimate the South African Oil Company could have reaped around seven US cents a barrel. In the first year of the contract that would have been worth about $1,4-million (R11,2-million at R8/dollar).

As of October 2000 the contract was extended for another year, and it was soon increased in volume to 120 000 barrels a day. That would translate to a profit of about $3-million (R24-million). The contract is still alive but, according to Lawal, since December 2001 the NNPC has been under-performing and has supplied only about 25% of the volume.

But to get back to the increase in volume after October 2000: in September that year, Nigerian newspapers reported that a delegation led by Thibedi Ramontja, then a senior official in South Africa's Department of Minerals and Energy, had applied to the NNPC to increase "South Africa's" allocation. Another case of South African state support for Lawal's company?

But what if the media got it wrong all along, mistakenly reporting that this was South Africa's contract and not Lawal's? Well, even Deputy President Jacob Zuma perpetuated the myth. In April 2001 he was quoted as saying during a parliamentary debate on bilateral relations: "It is also significant to note that Nigeria increased South Africa's crude oil allocation ... to 120 000 barrels a day."

Lawal confirmed this week that the South African state and pub-

lic have not benefited, maintaining that the contract was "a private commercial arrangement" between the NNPC and his company — in other words completely unrelated to the South African government.
30.05

Lawal gave the following reply through his lawyers, who stressed that the deal was a "private commercial arrangement" between Lawal's company and the Nigerian National Petroleum Corporation (NNPC):

"During 1999, and as occurs every year, the [NNPC] advertised in various newspapers an invitation for trading companies to apply to buy and lift Nigerian crude oil.

"Since the Camac Group had been operating, lifting crude and investing significantly with global energy firms in Nigeria for several years it applied for the right to buy and to lift Nigerian crude oil. It was one of some 18 trading companies who succeeded.

"The entity which applied for and obtained the above rights was South African Oil Company, a company registered in the Cayman Islands.

"It is important to note that the Camac Group has a full and proper infrastructure in the Cayman Islands. The reason for the reference to South Africa in the name of the Cayman company is that, at the appropriate time, the Cayman Group intended to extensively develop its oil interests in Africa, and particularly in South Africa.

"The Cayman company is not to be confused with South African Oil Company ... which is a company registered in South Africa but which does not trade, has no assets and, to all intents and purposes, is dormant ...

"The invitation by NNPC was to trading companies. The assertions relating to South Africa and/or its government [as the entity allocated the contract] are accordingly incorrect ...

"The South African company has never had any contractual or financial involvement in the above contract. It is a private commercial arrangement between the Cayman company and the NNPC.

"As far as our clients are aware, in 1999 the South African State President sent a letter to the President of Nigeria as a gesture of support of the Camac Group. It should not be ignored that, at that time, the Camac Group employed several hundred people in South Africa and intended to invest in South Africa, which it has done.

"At present the Camac Group employs approximately 1500 people in South Africa.

"[President Mbeki's] letter can hardly be given the generous interpretation of meaning that South African government officials were at various stages involved in attempts to secure the contract/securing increases in the volume of the contract ...

"No political party or politician in South Africa has ever benefited from the contracts. Similarly, no political party or politician in South Africa has benefited from donations by Mr Lawal and/or any entity within his group."

Hey, what's going on here?

Stefaans Brümmer and Sam Sole

Public life ends, by definition, where public officials go ostrich. When the people we elect to manage our nation's affairs refuse to account to us they break the pact of the ballot box. So it has been with the oil scandal.

A month ago the *Mail & Guardian* told how for the last four years a lucrative crude oil contract allocated by Nigeria to South Africa — described as a government-to-government deal — has benefited none but a private company registered in the Cayman Islands. Answers are due, but the silence has been proverbially deafening.

What, some have asked, is wrong here? It may help to recap. Crude oil is Nigeria's national asset and dominant export. There is intense competition among international oil companies for contracts to buy crude from the Nigerian National Petroleum Corporation (NNPC), the state oil company.

In 1999 President Thabo Mbeki lobbied directly with his Nigerian counterpart, Olusegun Obasanjo, for such a contract. The NNPC complied, allocating a substantial 55 000 barrels a day to "the Republic of South Africa". And after reported further lobbying the following year by a senior Department of Minerals and Energy official, the contract size was more than doubled to 120 000 barrels a day.

What should South Africa, or rather the public officials we elected to manage our nation's affairs, have done with the allocation? Simply, they should have used it in a way that benefited South Africa.

Most naturally they could have assigned it to the Central Energy Fund (CEF), which holds South Africa's state oil assets. The Strategic Fuel Fund Association (SFF), a company within the CEF group, could have dipped into it to augment our country's crude reserves stored at Saldanha Bay. (In November 2001 SFF bought 2-million barrels of Nigerian crude on the international market to replenish reserves. SFF may have obtained it more cheaply had it had access to the Nigerian allocation.)

What was left of the allocation the CEF group could have traded, or on-sold to a private company, for profit. That would have strengthened the CEF bottom line. As CEF is a national asset, the public good would have been served. An alternative option might have been to assign the allocation not to CEF, but to a private, South African company (preferably an empowerment company) after a transparent selection process. Publicly desirable objectives such as empowerment and an increase in the country's revenue base would have been achieved.

None of this happened. What did? Enter Camac, the United States-headquartered oil services group owned by Nigerian-American Kase Lawal and family. Camac created two companies with the same name — South African Oil Company (SAOC) — the one registered in South Africa and the other in the Cayman Islands, an offshore haven where secrecy laws facilitate corporate anonymity and tax avoidance.

Some time after the NNPC offered the allocation to "the Republic of South Africa" on August 16 1999, the Cayman-registered version of SAOC stepped in to sign. But that may not have been the original intention. Two days after the August 16 offer, the local version of SAOC (at the time urgently trying to have that name formally approved by the registrar of companies in Pretoria) had written to the NNPC to thank it for the allocation. The letter also referred to "our application submitted through the office of the President of the Republic of South Africa".

So it seems that Mbeki, or at least his office, knew that SAOC and not the South African state would benefit. The Presidency might not have known of the subsequent switch to the Cayman-registered company, but either scenario is deeply problematic. If the Presidency thought the contract was going to the South African version of SAOC, it might have justified it on the grounds that a local company with empowerment credentials was to benefit.

Indeed, Lawal had brought empowerment partners into the company: shares were earmarked for Provincial and Local Government Minister Sydney Mufamadi's wife, Nomusa; Eastern Cape Premier Makhenkesi Stofile's brother-in-law, Hintsa Siwisa; a charity headed by Stofile's wife, Nambita; a company co-owned by Stofile's sister-in-law, Nosipho Damasane; a company in which Limpopo Premier Ngoako Ramatlhodi's wife, Mathuding, had a stake; and finally Women's Development Bank Investment Holdings, its beneficiary trust chaired by First Lady Zanele Mbeki.

This is problematic for conflict-of-interest reasons, for how does one justify the expense of state effort, not least the president's personal efforts, to benefit a select group that reads like a who's who of interests close to the ruling party? The alternative, that the Presidency knew the Cayman version of SAOC would sign the contract, is equally problematic. Why secure a contract for South Africa only to have it taken up by a company that, in spite of its name, pays not a cent of taxes in South Africa?

But let's hear the other side: Camac and South Africa's Government Communication Information System have suggested that the allocation was never intended for South Africa; and that SAOC had won it fair and square from the NNPC. Besides, they maintained, what's wrong with a little political lobbying in the interests of bilateral trade? They're right, and wrong. They are right in the sense that yes, public officials do lobby abroad for the commercial interests of local companies. This is premised on the understanding that the local economy or bilateral trade relations are strengthened; a public good. But this argument becomes rickety when the outcome is considered: SAOC Cayman, which signed the contract, was not South African; the oil and the revenue stayed offshore; the local economy did not benefit; bilateral trade was unaffected.

But where they are dead wrong is the suggestion that this was an ordinary commercial deal. It was not. Neither the two SAOCs nor their parent company, the US-headquartered Camac, would have won the contract on commercial terms. The NNPC had earmarked most of its allocations to go to large-volume international traders and refining companies, neither of which described Camac, SAOC Cayman or SAOC South Africa. But the NNPC did make a handful of allocations to governments. Recently the NNPC confirmed that it regarded the South African contract as "government-to-government".

The only conclusion on the available facts is that the South African government reassigned, or allowed to be reassigned, South Africa's right to Nigerian oil to SAOC. Something that was of value to the South African state and public has benefited neither. Why? Before the *M&G* first published the story a month ago, Mbeki's office said the president would respond once he had investigated the facts. Neither Mbeki, nor the line-function Ministry of Minerals and Energy, has offered any explanation since.

In the absence of official response, gossip flourishes. Scenarios from the rumour-mill include that the ANC treasury or an individual politician gets a cut. There are some markers pointing in this general direction. Miles Nzama, an ANC fund-raiser, is listed as a director of SAOC South Africa. Nzama's principal, ANC treasurer-general Mendi Msimang, has refused to say whether his party benefits.

And then there is the mystery quarter-share. SAOC South Africa is 75% owned by the Camac group and its local empowerment partners. SAOC in the Caymans is 75% owned by the Camac group. In both countries 25% is not declared. On a conservative estimate the deal has generated a profit of R48-million over the last four years: R12-million for the mystery shareholder.

If the gossip is accurate and the ANC or an individual politician benefits, part of an asset allocated to South Africa has gone to a partisan or personal interest. There is only one word for that: kickback.

The public officials we elected to manage our nation's affairs owe an explanation lest the gossip stands. **20.06**

> **"The media must once again become an instrument of liberation by being reflective, critical and a partisan of the truth."**
> — President Thabo Mbeki, speaking at the first conference of African editors in South Africa on the role of the media . 17.04

It all started here

Stefaans Brümmer

Two and a half years ago a humble paragraph in the *Mail & Guardian* set in motion a train of events that led the Scorpions to focus on Jacob Zuma's role in the arms deal.

That was the genesis of an investigation that has culminated in the deputy president fighting for his political life, implicated in corruption alongside his comradely financial adviser, Schabir Shaik.

A reconstruction of events shows that Shaik probably has himself to blame, as much as anyone else, for his and Zuma's current predicament. Shaik's recklessness in matters of fact and of interpersonal relations, some would say, is what cooked their goose.

In January 2001, with allegations about corruption in the arms acquisition swirling, the *M&G* turned its focus on Shaik and his Nkobi group of companies, empowerment partners to French arms firm Thomson CSF (now called Thales).

Under the headline "New evidence of ANC arms deal link" the *M&G* raised questions about the apparent proximity of the Nkobi group to the African National Congress and individual ANC politicians. Among other things, that article contained a paragraph containing a list of supposed Nkobi Holdings shareholders as confirmed by Shaik. Well, Shaik's list was not accurate, and that set the cat among the pigeons. Among those listed by Shaik were the Workers' College (a union training facility) and the family of late ANC treasurer general Thomas Nkobi (after whom Shaik's group was named). Their "shareholding" was news to both.

A week later the *M&G* carried the outraged reaction of Workers' College representatives, one of whom said he smelt "a very big and very dirty rat", and of the Nkobi family, which was "distressed". The Nkobis retained Johannesburg lawyer Ian Jordaan to pursue Shaik's apparent abuse of the family name. Jordaan and the Nkobis went as high as President Thabo Mbeki to get clarification, with little success. During the course of this, luminaries such as late defence minister Joe Modise popped up on the Shaik side of negotiations. Zuma's looming presence alongside Shaik became increasingly apparent.

It is understood that a member of National Director of Public

Prosecutions Bulelani Ngcuka's staff, after conversations with Jordaan, took a special interest in Zuma's role. There were other factors that spurred the interest of Ngcuka's investigator, such as a trip or trips by Zuma and Shaik to Malaysia, but the information unlocked from the Jordaan conversations was the "main thing" that led the Scorpions to train their sights on Zuma. Which is not to say that it would not have happened anyway, for by that time another set of events was unfolding that would soon reach the investigators' attention. And, again, Shaik had himself as much as anyone else to blame.

A few months earlier, in November 2000, Shaik had allegedly convened a meeting with Thomson/Thales representatives in Mauritius, where, among other things, discussions turned to "damage control" in relation to media allegations of arms deal corruption. There, a Shaik employee was privy to some of the talk. That female employee, and others, soon left Shaik's employ because of what may be termed "interpersonal" problems. They were ripe for the picking as witnesses.

But not necessarily keen. An earlier affidavit by William Downer, one of Ngcuka's investigators, speaks of evidence being obtained under oath from "two very scared and reluctant witnesses. Both indicated their wish not to get involved in the matter and had to be summonsed and compelled to testify." One had been paid a R40 000 settlement by the Nkobi group when she left its employ, but she also had to sign confidentiality agreements presented to her by Shaik's attorney who, according to Downer's affidavit, told her this was because she "knew too much about the relationship" between Shaik and Zuma. At least two of these witnesses did eventually cooperate with investigators. They may even have had "insurance" that became useful documentary evidence.

And so the Scorpions learnt of the March 2000 encrypted fax in which a Thomson/Thales representative told his colleagues about Zuma's "confirmation" of an alleged request for a R500 000 annual bribe. This information led investigators, some time before or during August 2001, to the Thomson offices in Midrand, where they seized documents that seemed to corroborate the request.

In October that year Ngcuka's investigators raided Nkobi, Shaik and Thomson/Thales premises in South Africa and, with judicial assistance, abroad. The documentation obtained seemed to indicate a *prima facie* corruption case against Shaik, Thomson/Thales or some of its employees, and Zuma. The investigation was pursued in secret, to the extent that Downer's affidavit (made to obtain the October search warrants) referred to Zuma as "Mr X". But the *M&G* saw through that. Last November we headlined: "Arms 'bribe': Scorpions investigate Jacob Zuma". The rest is history. **29.08**

Madiba, we thank you

Editorial

So, for what shall we thank Nelson Mandela? Shall we thank him for all those months he spent on the run criss-crossing the country and, like an elusive rabbit, dashing into the nearest hole at the sign of danger? Shall we thank him for the years he spent breaking stones on Robben Island, paying the price for daring to stand up to white supremacy?

Shall we thank him for seeing the need — when the rest of us had resigned ourselves to the inevitability of a gargantuan showdown — to avert bloodshed and shepherd his comrades and enemies towards a negotiated settlement? Shall we rather tell him of our gratitude for the sternness and grace with which he led us through those first five years of democracy, during which he taught us the values of forgiveness and the primacy of nation-building? Or shall we tell him how grateful we are for the icon and moral compass he has continued to be when he could be enjoying his twilight years and patting himself on the back for a job well done?

Yes, we should thank him for all these things. But our most heartfelt gratitude should be reserved for the fact that he has lived in our times, *Homo sapiens* with a colossus against which we more fragile mortals can measure ourselves.

Through the ages, the human race has had its icons — men and women who rose above ordinariness to inspire their generations. They have given to their generational peers the wisdom and the tools needed to advance the human condition.

In our generation the gods bequeathed us Nelson Mandela, who for billions around the world has come to symbolise the virtues and values needed to reverse the barbarism that characterised human behaviour in the past century. Mandela emerged from prison towards the end of a century marked by two world wars, a Holocaust, genocides and bloody civil conflicts to provide a new moral light. He took a country whose political system had embodied the worst excesses of Nazism, capitalism, communism and racism and turned it into the world's moral beacon. He preached and lived reconciliation and nation-building. He also taught us the virtues of humility and caring, never missing the opportunity of trekking to far-off corners to visit a dying cancer sufferer or to spend time with the vulnerable and downtrodden classes.

In post-retirement Mandela has continued to play his role as the international moral voice, speaking about such outrages as the United States's war on Iraq and as a voice for the voiceless, waging battle on behalf of HIV-positive South Africans. He has a spontaneity that is missing from the bland, manufactured and scripted leaders who dominate the world scene. It is only he who can tell George W Bush what most of the world thinks of his mental capacity. It is only he who has no qualms about telling Africa's political dinosaurs about the destruction they are wreaking on the continent. And it is only he who has the courage to prick the cold conscience of the business sector.

In celebrating Madiba — South Africa's precious gift to the world — let us remember to tell him all these things while he lives. Let us remember to tell him — even though he will strenuously resist this — that he is, for this generation of humanity, what many of the great prophets and philosophers of previous aeons were to their generations. And while he lives let us remember to tell him: Madiba, we thank you. **18.07**

LETTER

Madiba, a true world leader

Recent statements by Nelson Mandela illustrate why democrats worldwide hold him in high esteem — for his reverence for the rule of law and a preparedness to speak out against its abuse. At the African National Congress's December congress, Mandela criticised his party for being in charge of a government seemingly neglectful of its electoral mandate.

In the past week Mandela has turned his moral wrath on the United States, whose president, with the connivance of the sycophantic British Prime Minister Tony Blair, seems hell-bent on blowing Iraq to smithereens, ahead of the findings of the United Nations inspectors' report. For the democrat Mandela, not only does this badgering of the UN by the US fly in the face of the sovereignty of the august world body and international law — in arrogant defiance of the world's desire for peace — it is close to being a racist slur against the UN's African leader, Kofi Annan.

We all know what is at stake. With or without oil, Iraq is impoverished. With or without weapons of mass destruction, it stands no chance against the combined military power of the US and Britain. Saddam Hussein's bravado is a tragicomic buffoonery given the loss of life about to befall Iraq's wretched citizenry.

Mandela has proven himself to be an "old school" democrat with a lawyer's sensitivity to any attempt to undermine the sovereignty of the people, whether by local politicians or warmongering foreign superpowers. That is the reason for having the UN in the first place, that we may live in a safer world. — *Moji Mokone, Johannesburg, 14.02*

LETTER: IN BRIEF

The SABC recently televised the movie *Mandela and De Klerk*, and I was elated that Nelson Mandela's life was filmed so that the new generation can catch up with our history. But why was Sydney Poitier chosen to play the role of Mandela? Poitier's accent is too American, and his voice was not authoritative and commanding. The two have nothing in common except height. Do we really have to use Americans to tell South African stories? — *Thabile Mange, Kagiso, 20.03*

> **"Don't assume he wants to meet me. I know he's coming to meet President Mbeki."** — Nelson Mandela, about US President George W Bush's visit to South Africa. Mandela had earlier made derogatory remarks about Bush's intelligence. Bush did not visit Mandela. 04.07

We must not fear to dream

Editorial

Some may find it odd that many in South Africa are this week celebrating the birthday of an organisation that does not exist. Others, who were much closer to the United Democratic Front (UDF), would find it odd that the 20th anniversary celebrations are, in fact, so muted, given the impact of that organisation on the country's history.

It all depends where you come from. Those who were part of the UDF and its allied organisations know it was the vehicle that turned a lethargic anti-apartheid effort into a highly mobile mass-based struggle. Reviving mass organisation in the post-Rivonia and post-1977 crushing of the freedom struggle, the UDF employed tactics and strategies that were to ensure that the Nats would never again be allowed to fully silence opposition.

Sadly, the UDF legacy has faded into historical obscurity and that famous acronym is hardly ever mentioned when stories of triumph over apartheid are told. The UDF presided over a golden era in the South African liberation struggle. It was an era in which the language of Trevor Manuel was one of organisational rather than fiscal discipline, when Mosiuoa (don't we all miss Terror?) Lekota led mass formations rather than military formations, when Cyril Ramaphosa wrestled with Bobby Godsell over the upliftment of the working classes instead of hopping off to sign the next empowerment deal.

It was a glorious time, when we dreamed brave dreams: of freedom, of equality and — dare we say it today? — of socialism. It was also a brutal time, when PW Botha made sure those dreams were tampered with. Thousands were imprisoned, tortured and killed during that era as the National Party regime saw its rope get shorter and shorter. Others simply disappeared, their bones only to be unearthed by the Truth and Reconciliation Commission, while many still remain unaccounted for.

Yet the spirit that drove the leaders, members and supporters of the UDF was not broken. Dreams continued to be dreamed, battles continued to be fought. And thus was kept alive the faith of the people of South Africa that the prison bars would be broken and the exiles would return home to build a caring republic.

The unique legacy of the UDF should serve as an inspiration to oppressed peoples everywhere. The tactics and strategies of this formation should compel the Zimbabwean and Swazi people to realise that they will not remove their despotic leaders by wailing and lamely appealing for outside pressure to be applied. It should also inspire the people of Palestine, Burma and Saharawi to believe that oppression and injustice do not always triumph in the end.

Cynics will argue that to lament the UDF is to romanticise a bygone era. We all know that the world has changed and that the tactics of the anti-apartheid struggle cannot be transplanted into a free society. We cannot today expect clergymen to preach revolution in places of worship, youths to stand at street corners debating Gramsci, or our artists to produce "relevant" works. That would be to negate the achievements of the liberation struggle.

For us, in a post-liberation South Africa seeking its soul again, a glimpse back to the UDF era shows us those qualities and values that we should entrench and carry forward: free thought, non-racialism, the ability to challenge authority, the value of participatory democracy and encouragement of the multiplicity of ideas. And as we head towards the second decade of our democracy we should recapture the spirit that enabled us not to fear dreaming. **22.08**

LETTER
Once were warriors

Minister of Health Manto Tshabalala-Msimang wore a beautiful hat to the opening of Parliament. Crafted in a billowing black fabric, it flared upward and around in a confection that prettily framed her Purdy-inspired, bobbed wig.

A pity the minister didn't use the ample shade it would have provided on the podium of the Treatment Action Campaign (TAC) march later that day, when the February sun began to scorch. The black hat and the minister's red couture dress would have contrasted so well with the marchers' purple T-shirts saying "HIV Positive" and the little white coffins they carried. Each coffin bore testimony to a child that could have been saved with drug treatment.

This Aids movement is one born of African National Congress loins, successfully appropriating its struggle culture. A group of young men toyi-toyied on the tarmac outside the "people's Parliament", which had its black iron gates shut tight.

This is a younger, less patient generation than its parents. And while its call is for society to galvanise itself for this new struggle, that call can so easily spill over into so many other political campaigns. And this generation has its own new heroes — young activists queued for a photograph with the TAC's Zackie Achmat.

The ANC should watch out when it slights this "single issue" campaign as orchestrated by a few whiteys in the grip of avaricious drug multinationals.

The purple sea filled the street as far as the eye could see, with people who live with the virus, priests, doctors, nurses, students, clothing workers and the former MP Pregs Govender, who has unshackled herself from public office to find her voice.

ANC MP and workhorse Barbara Hogan, thankfully, had not lost hers. "When the people march on Parliament in these numbers, government cannot ignore what is being said," she told the marchers. "Amandla!" came the reply.

At the anti-war march the next day, Deputy Minister of Defence Nozizwe Madlala-Routledge wore an ANC peaked cap (no hat), baggy pants, struggle T-shirt, no bodyguard. "Down with Bush," she chanted. This was more the ANC I know: a party of the people; that when facing a battle fights it. And one that is not so imperiously distant from its grassroots as the one on display at the Aids march.

At the anti-war march was Ronnie Kasrils, draped in his Palestinian revolutionary scarf. Kader Asmal was there; so was Penuell Maduna and Pallo Jordan.

Ja, this is the ANC I *smaak*, I thought. The mad hatters have not yet triumphed over the peaked caps.

But then a nagging thought that won't go away: where were they the day before, at another march to fight another war? — *Ferial Haffajee, Johannesburg, 28.02*

The long walk to civil disobedience

Zackie Achmat

When my comrades and I disrupted Minister of Health Manto Tshabalala-Msimang's speech at the Health Systems Trust conference last week, a public health official taunted one of the Treatment Action Campaign (TAC) members by saying: "How did you get HIV anyway?" We also received an angry letter from a man who feels our demand for treatment is unfair. This article is written for them. It is also written for people like Western Cape African National Congress health spokesperson, Cameron Dugmore, who called us bullies for disrupting the minister.

First, I apologise unconditionally to the minister for referring to her personal appearance during our disruption. Any reference to the personal appearance of an opponent to discredit them is wrong. It's also wrong because it undermines the dignity of the protest of thousands of TAC volunteers and allows people who need to curry favour with officials a cover for their lack of courage and morality. It is also no excuse to say that I was angry, because a few minutes before my own anger against indifference became uncontrollable I had told a comrade whose mother had been hospitalised with a CD4 count of 54 and raging tuberculosis that she should use her anger to demonstrate peacefully.

But there are many things I do not apologise for. I do not apologise for holding Tshabalala-Msimang and Minister of Trade and Industry Alec Erwin responsible for thousands of HIV/Aids deaths. Second, neither the TAC nor I will make any apology for making the minister of health, any politician or bureaucrat feel uncomfortable through a disruption of any meeting, office or event where they may find themselves. Hundreds of premature, painful, awkward, silent and screaming deaths of children, men and women daily are caused by the failure of the government to implement a comprehensive treatment and prevention plan for HIV/Aids.

To Dugmore and the other detractors of our campaign who call us bullies, let me ask: Were you at the many lawful marches to

Parliament to give memoranda to the minister and the president begging for HIV treatment? Perhaps you did not see our march of about 15 000 people on the South African Parliament asking the government to sign a treatment and prevention plan on February 14? What about our earlier pickets of Parliament, drug companies and the United States government?

Civil disobedience is action of last resort for us, because exhaustive efforts at engagement have not worked. Let me ask further: did you attend any of more than 10 submissions to various parliamentary portfolio committees begging, cajoling, charming and arguing for HIV treatment? Did you attend any of more than 30 interfaith services held by the TAC and our allies across the country appealing to the conscience of the health minister and the government? Do you know that we tried quietly to persuade Dr Ayanda Ntsaluba, Dr Nono Simelela, Dr Essop Jassat, Dr Ismail Cachalia, Dr Saadiq Kariem, Dr Kammy Chetty, Dr Abe Nkomo and other doctors who are members of the ANC to ensure that the government change its policies or to let their scientific training, their Hippocratic oaths and their consciences allow them to speak the truth? Maybe you also tried to persuade them that real loyalty to the ANC and the ideals of the Freedom Charter required open criticism after numerous private pleas? Have you reminded the ministers of health and trade and industry that they are undermining the ANC's traditions of freedom, equality, solidarity and dignity?

Do you remember that the health minister and her supporters in Cabinet really represent the anti-democratic traditions of the former Stalinist states that supported them? Perhaps one should expect people who denied the existence of the Gulag or applauded the invasion of Czechoslovakia, Hungary, Poland and East Germany by Soviet troops and called the latest Zimbabwean election legitimate to deny the existence of HIV/Aids and the efficacy of anti-retrovirals?

Did you attend hundreds of community meetings addressed by TAC volunteers across the country to educate ourselves and our people about HIV, prevention and treatment? Did you help late into the night, in support of the government, to develop a court case against the drug companies to reduce the prices of all medicines including HIV/Aids medicines? Do you remember how the health minister spurned the TAC after the case?

Do you know the anguish of the person who made the poster that said: "Thabo your ideas are toxic"? Were you at the funeral of Queenie Qiza (one of the first TAC volunteers) or did you hear Christopher Moraka choke to death after appealing to Parliament to reduce the prices of medicines? Maybe, like me, you avoided the funeral of my cousin Farieda because I cannot face the pain of death? Did you feel as encouraged as we were by the Cabinet statement of April 17 2002? Are you as disappointed a year later that so little has been done? Were you there when we illegally imported a good quality generic antifungal drug (Fluconazole) and shamed drug company Pfizer for profiteering?

Maybe you followed the TAC/Congress of South African Trade Unions's treatment congress where unemployed people, nurses, scientists, cleaners and trade unionists invited the government to develop a treatment plan? Do you remember our meeting with Deputy President Jacob Zuma that led to a promise that a treatment and prevention plan would be developed by the end of February 2003?

Did you miss the word-games played by the government over negotiations at the National Economic and Development Labour Council (Nedlac)? Are you one of the people who phone Nedlac regularly to hear when the government will return to the negotiating table? Or, are you one of the people too busy taking care of someone dying but who have a little pride in your heart when an activist says to the president: "Comrade, you are not listening to our cries. You are denying the cause of our illness. You are not helping us get medicines."

After countless attempts at talking, public pressure and even a court case to prevent HIV infection from mother-to-child, the government allows the deaths to continue while it plays the caring, right-minded diplomat in Africa and the Middle East. Politeness disguises the moral and legal culpability of these politicians and officials. We believe that the personal crises faced by many of our families, friends, nurses, doctors, colleagues and their children should be turned into discomfort and a crisis for the politicians and bureaucrats who continue to deny our people medicine.

The fact that the health minister is obstructing the departments of health, finance, labour and the deputy president's office from signing and implementing a treatment and prevention plan costs our society more than 600 lives and many new HIV infections every day. The government uses Parliament, Cabinet, provincial governments and all its resources including the Government Communication and Information Service, in the person of comrade Joel Netshitenze, or health communications officer, Joanne Collinge, to justify its denial of life-saving medicines to people who need them. It uses these resources to protect the reputation of the minister of health. And you add your voices to their chorus? When will you join reason, passion and anger to win treatment for people living with HIV/Aids and a decent public health system for all?

The TAC will win in this campaign because its members act in good faith. And when we win, we will sit down on any day with the government for as long as it takes to tackle all the difficult problems of HIV/Aids and the health system. These wounds between ourselves and the government will not be healed easily. But they will heal easier than the pain of the millions who are denied life-saving treatment and those who have succumbed to that pain. **04.04**

Zackie Achmat is the Treatment Action Campaign's chairperson

The madness of Queen Manto

Nawaal Deane

Minister of Health Manto Tshabalala-Msimang this week launched an extraordinary racial attack against the Treatment Action Campaign (TAC) at a formal gala event. Guests at the event, who heard the attack, included United Nations emissaries, diplomats, leading academics and corporate captains.

The health minister was speaking at a welcoming ceremony for Richard Feachem, the executive director of the Global Fund for HIV/Aids, TB and Malaria, on Tuesday evening when she launched the attack on TAC chairman Mark Heywood from the podium, accusing him — "a white man" — of masterminding the civil disobedience campaign against the government and her.

Feachem is on an official visit to South Africa. He had hoped to sign a $41-million grant to the country. But, at the time of going to press, the deal was apparently in doubt. Feachem controls the UN fund, which has a budget of $3,4-billion to disperse to countries to fight the epidemics.

The evening began in a civil manner, with officials from the Department of Health, church leaders and members of the business sector having cocktails at the posh Summer Place in Hyde Park. Outside the gates, a handful of TAC members had gathered to protest against the government's ambivalence over the provision of a national anti-retroviral treatment programme. Holding red "Wanted" posters of Tshabalala-Msimang and Minister of Trade and Industry Alec Erwin, the group chanted when cars drove through the gates.

Things rapidly deteriorated when Tshabalala-Msimang stepped on to the podium. She began to explain why she had sneaked into the gala event through the back entrance. She was meant to be introducing Feachem and welcoming his delegation, but as there was "some kind of demonstration outside" her bodyguards had feared for her safety. "I came through the back door but I would want one of you to invite these people to join us ... to listen to what we have to say."

She then launched into a blistering, sarcastic attack that left senior government officials, Feachem and the rest of the high-profile audience cringing. "They come with two buses and go to the commissions where they wait for the white man to tell them what to do ... Our Africans say: 'Let's us wait for a white man to deploy us ... to say to us ... you must toyi toyi here.'"

Tshabalala-Msimang said the campaigners had gone to the Human Rights Commission with placards of the two "murderers" in the country. The posters say that the two ministers are "wanted for not stopping 600 HIV/Aids deaths every day". Nono Simelela, chief director of the HIV/Aids unit, dropped her head, while Gauteng MEC for Health Gwen Ramokgopa averted her eyes from the stunned audience.

Representatives of Global Fund grant recipients from *Soul City* and loveLife looked from Tshabalala-Msimang at the podium, to Heywood, who was standing directly in her line of sight behind the seated guests, as if they were watching a tennis match. Heywood was the only member of the TAC at the function because he was on the University of the Witwatersrand's guest list.

The minister was referring to part of the civil disobedience campaign where 200 predominantly African women went to both the Gender Commission and Human Rights Commission last week to hand over memorandums demanding that these constitutional organisations stand up for the rights of those living with HIV/Aids. Neither organisation has entered the fray on HIV/Aids, though it falls within their ambit.

Tshabalala-Msimang spoke of Heywood as a white director holding sway over a group of impotent black actors. Without referring to him by name she said that this "white man" was among the guests. Feachem looked bemused at Tshabalala-Msimang's continuous reference to this "white man". Heywood was clearly furious. "You are lying, minister," he retaliated. There was a deathly silence until Tshabalala-Msimang thanked him for speaking up, saying she was happy she did not have to mention him by name. "You are a liar," he shouted as she continued to speak above him through the microphone.

Tshabalala-Msimang's burly bodyguard went up to Heywood and told him not to talk back to the minister. Then, as if nothing unusual had occurred, the minister went on with her speech while Feachem and his delegation looked on in embarrassed silence. She contradicted Feachem's calls for proposals to finance anti-retroviral treatment, saying the South African National Aids Council (Sanac), the Global Fund's country coordinating mechanism, saying, "For the third round of proposals Sanac will put forward issues of nutrition and traditional herbal remedies."

She pointedly ignored references to anti-retroviral (ARV) treatment, again contradicting the Cabinet's stated policy — to find ways of extending ARV treatment by making it cost effective through co-financing with the Global Fund. The minister then blamed the Global Fund for delaying the South African grant. She said: "We had hoped to sign the agreement, but there are a few loose ends. The reason we have not moved with speed is because the Global Fund had to set their house in order and not that Sanac was not ready. Geneva was not ready." Part of the reason for the delay was that a separate R700-million grant was awarded to the Enhancing Care Initiative, a KwaZulu-Natal organisation. The proposal had a large ARV component and was delayed because the KwaZulu-Natal proposal had not gone through Sanac.

Speaking after Tshabalala-Msimang, Feachem did not refer to her comments but called on all sectors to apply to the fund for co-financing of ARV therapy. He said: "It would be foolish of me not to be aware of the controversy around anti-retroviral treatment." But he pointed out that ARV programmes are inevitable and are already operating in the country. A source in Feachem's delegation said he had been angered by the minister's racist comments. Heywood left the gathering immediately after Feachem's speech.

The *Mail & Guardian* was informed that Tshabalala-Msimang's spokesperson, Sibani Mngadi, was trying to find out which journalists had attended the cocktail party and witnessed the incident. **11.04**

The Global Fund deal was later signed, in August 2003.

The dead hand of denialism

Edwin Cameron

My theme touches on two momentous issues from the past century. The first is the Holocaust — the Nazi state's methodical extinction during World War II of approximately six million people, mostly Jews. The second is the Aids pandemic — the global pandemic of disease and death, particularly in Africa and the developing world, resulting from infection with HIV.

Each in different ways seems emblematic of the past century's terrible legacy of human vulnerability and failing — the Holocaust because of what it says about the capacity of supposedly cultivated humans to commit systematised murder on a vast scale; Aids because of what it seems to be saying about the incapacity of supposedly cultivated humans for systematised intervention, within their means, to prevent avoidable death from disease on a massive scale in the developing world.

No one here would, I think, deny that nearly six million Jews, together with gypsies, homosexuals and other outcasts, were systematically done to death in German concentration camps during World War II. Nor would anyone deny that a virally specific contagious condition, mostly sexually transmitted, is ravaging the heterosexual populations of Central and Southern Africa. Yet both these facts are denied — persistently, vigorously, vehemently, and sometimes venomously.

For denialists, the facts are unacceptable. They therefore set out to render them untrue. They engage in radical controversion, for ideological purposes, of facts that, by and large, are accepted by almost all experts and lay persons as having been established on the basis of overwhelming evidence.

Holocaust denialism seeks to deny the systematised massacre of the Jews of continental Europe that took place during World War II. Aids denialism involves a group of dissident historians, social commentators and scientists who have set about denying the forbidding fact of Aids. Denialists assert that the "hypothesis" that Aids is caused by a sexually transmitted virus is unproven and irresponsible. Aids in North America and Western European they attribute to "the long-term consumption of recreational drugs" and to the widespread use of drugs as sexual stimulants by homosexual men and, more recently, to the administration of anti-retroviral drugs that doctors wrongly prescribe for Aids. They refute the "impression" that there is a microbial epidemic in Africa, ascribing it instead to "non-contagious risk factors that are limited to certain sub-sets of the African population". The millions of deaths attributed to Aids they characterise as "a minor fraction of conventional mortality under a new name".

The methods each group employs to controvert the facts include distortions, half-truths, misrepresentation of their opponents' positions and expedient shifts of premises and logic. The denialists' "standard recipe" is described on one Holocaust website as "the half-truth, the distortion, and quite a lot besides the truth".

Both forms of denial make great play of the inescapable indeterminacy of figures and statistics. Precisely how many died at Auschwitz, and of what causes? Exactly how many HIV infections and Aids deaths are current in Africa? We shall probably never know. Denialists seek to suggest that the inability to achieve historical or epidemiological exactitude renders the Holocaust and Aids themselves imaginary.

Both rely, spuriously, on the fact that history is replete with orthodoxies that have been supplanted by the heterodox, and invoke the memory of Galileo Galilei, who was nearly martyred for scientific truth. The analogy could be invoked by every non-Galilean absurdist to advance his or her theory. The difference is that heterodoxies that have achieved acceptance have complied with the basic logic of scientific and evidentiary postulates, whereas it is precisely these qualities that the denialists' assertions lack.

In each debate the antagonists need to account for their opponents' conduct. Why, if the Holocaust never happened, would many thousands of reputable historians commit themselves to the assertion that it did? Why would more than 5 000 HIV/Aids specialist physicians and scientists from 82 countries subscribe to a declaration — as they did in the Durban Declaration of June 2000 — that the evidence that HIV causes Aids is "clear-cut, exhaustive and unambiguous"?

To explain this, denialists in each case resort to conspiratorialism. In the case of the Holocaust, Jewish historians and Holocaust specialists have a close-knit racial interest in fabricating its existence.

In the case of Aids, many scientists are mere fools, trapped in dogmatic error. But all too many of them have a baser motive. According to Professor Peter Duesberg, the "deceptive Aids propaganda" alleging the existence of a microbial Aids epidemic in Africa has been "introduced and inspired by new American biotechnology", one that — at least in the case of HIV testing — "provides job security" for virologists and doctors, "without ever producing any public health benefits".

African Aids denialism also employs a theory of racial conspiracy. The deniers depict the facts about Aids as the product of a grotesque racist conspiracy of untruth and deception by corporations, doctors, scientists and healthcare workers — a monstrous plot against Africans because they are black.

A document of disputed authorship, which was distributed last year under the authority of the ruling party in South Africa, the African National Congress, propagates the belief that a syndicate of white Western interests — an "omnipotent apparatus", engaged in "a massive political-commercial campaign to promote anti-retroviral drugs" — seeks to degrade, exploit and by the administration to them of toxic medicines, kill, Africans.

For South Africa, the significance of Aids denialism is momentous. It has to be, since our president, President Thabo Mbeki, has publicly countenanced and officially encouraged it. The president's stand has caused predictable confusion and dismay among ordinary South Africans — with unavoidably devastating consequences in an epidemic where public education about self-protection and the necessity for behaviour change is a life-saving centrality.

But more important still, it has bedevilled and unfortunately continues to bedevil our national response to the disease. Instead of taking immediate and unflinching action to stem the epidemic and to minimise the devastation it is wreaking, the government has continued to respond with ambivalence and inaction and distraction and evasion.

For some time Mbeki has maintained silence in regard to his endorsement or otherwise of the Aids denialists. Yet in one of his rare references to Aids earlier this year, he described it as a disease "of poverty and underdevelopment" — echoing one of the key dogmas of denialism.

In January 2003 his Minister of Health, Manto Tshabalala-Msimang, invited a prominent Aids denialist, Dr Robert Giraldo, to address the meeting of the Southern Africa Development Community's ministerial health committee, which she chairs. Giraldo, unsurprisingly, informed the meeting that "the transmission of Aids from person to person is a myth" and that "the homosexual transmission of the epidemic in Western countries, as well as the heterosexual transmission in Africa, is an assumption made without any scientific validation". The government has now apparently retained his services to advise it on "nutrition". Recently the Minister of Finance, Trevor Manuel, doubtless unwittingly, echoed dissident talk by accusing proponents of anti-retroviral treatment of speaking "a lot of voodoo" and "bunkum".

Until September 2002 the most the government would say was that its policies were based on the "assumption" that HIV causes Aids. Even now, government will still say no more than that its policies are based on the "premise" that HIV causes Aids. The ambiguity of expression, the ambivalence of the underlying belief, the doubt about the commitment, are all too tragically apparent. It is as if a formerly avowed racist were to undertake to treat black people on the "assumption" or "premise" that they are his equals.

Some advocate criminal proscription of Holocaust denial, and several states have prohibited speech that denies events associated with the Nazi persecution of the Jews. The motivation is that these laws proscribe "hate speech" with its attendant injury to the human rights protections of those whom it deliberately targets.

But many have misgivings about the efficacy and justification of these laws, considering that they may be counter-productive, and that they obscure the role that public debate, refutation and education should play in resisting untruth. A second role that the law can play, however, is as an arbiter of fact and truth. And civil, rather than criminal, litigation may offer useful strategies in responding to denialism.

Holocaust and Aids denialism have each recently been challenged in court, with momentous consequences. In the Royal Courts of Justice in the Strand, in London between January 11 and April 11 2000, the trial matter between David Irving, plaintiff, and the defendants Penguin Books and Deborah Lipstadt was conducted before Mr Justice Gray. The case arose from a libel suit the writer David Irving brought against the defendants for publishing Lipstadt's assertions that Irving was a "Holocaust denier" who had distorted historical materials in order to bolster Hitler's reputation.

The trial resulted in the dismissal of the plaintiff's claim and the vindication of the defendants' assertions about the plaintiff, including their claim that Irving was an anti-Semite. Even more importantly, the dispute required the trial judge to make detailed historical findings regarding the Holocaust and the central areas of difference between Holocaust historians and denialists.

Justice Gray's judgement scrutinises the contentions at the centre of the deniers' claims, and finds them wanting not only in force but in integrity. His conclusions entail that those who persist in denying the Holocaust are devoid of professional integrity and lack commitment to truth. Of particular interest to the broader issue of denialism are his findings in relation to the "convergence" of Irving's historiographical errors. He found they all tended to exonerate Hitler, and to reflect Irving's partisanship for the Nazi leader. "If indeed they were genuine errors or mistakes, one would not expect to find this consistency." The judge concluded that this was a cogent reason for supposing that Irving had deliberately slanted the evidence.

The same pattern of convergence marks the "errors" of Aids denialists. Eleven months to the day after Mbeki began his public endorsement of the Aids denialists, the Constitutional Court delivered a judgement in a case involving discrimination by a state agency against a work-seeker with HIV. Even though the medical issues were undisputed on appeal, the court went out of its way, in a pointed exercise in public education and affirmation, to set out in detail the uncontested scientific evidence that HIV is the cause of Aids.

Eighteen months later the Constitutional Court was confronted with one of its largest challenges since the transition to democracy — the government's refusal to introduce a national programme to counter transmission of HIV from pregnant mothers to their infants. Although exhaustively documented evidence supports the efficacy, attainability and simple monetary good sense of such programmes — leaving aside the humane imperative for them —and even though the drugs are available free, the government refused to implement such a programme.

Its refusal, as documented in its court papers and in argument on its behalf before the high court and Constitutional Court, was based in large measure on the alleged toxicity of the drugs — a tenet central to the entire conspiratorialist theory of the Aids denialists. Invoking its exposition in its earlier judgment of the causes of Aids, the court held there was no evidence to suggest that a dose of the anti-retroviral drug in question "to both mother and child at the time of birth will result in harm to either of them".

Observing that Aids was "the greatest threat to public health in our country", the Court ruled that the Constitution required the government to devise and implement within its available resources "a comprehensive and coordinated programme to realise progressively the rights of pregnant woman and their newborn children to have access to health services to combat mother-to-child transmission of HIV".

The Constitutional Court's judgements assert that irrationality and obfuscation have no place in South Africa's response to the worst threat to its national life. It has directed the government onto a road that, if followed, would lead to the effective and coherent national response to the epidemic. There is unfortunately little evidence that the government has taken the path on to which the court has beckoned it.

Despite two important and hopeful Cabinet statements in April and October 2002, there is increasingly a dualism between governmental statement and action concerning Aids. The evidence points to the dismal conclusion that the dead hand of denialism still weighs down all too heavily on the development of a rational and effective response to Aids.

Although HIV is now a medically manageable condition, the government still refuses to commit itself to a national treatment plan for Aids — even though late last year substantial progress was made in negotiations between business, NGOs and the heads of two government departments in devising such a plan.

The cost in human lives and suffering of denialist-inspired equivocation in national Aids policy can be described only as horrendous. A leading Aids activist, Zackie Achmat, has referred to government's policies — with resonant imagery — as "a Holocaust against the poor". Death from Aids is now avoidable. With carefully administered treatments, and subject to monitoring and with appropriate medical care, Aids is no longer a fatal disease. I know this from my own life, which without those treatments would have ended three or more years ago. Neither as a person living with Aids nor as a judge can I stand apart from the struggle for truth and for action about Aids, and the role lawyers and the legal system are called to play in it.

Both Holocaust and Aids denial remind us of our own terrible weaknesses and vulnerabilities as humans, and of the reluctance we all feel to own them. But the struggle for truth they involve also inspires us to greater thought and action. For truth, classically, is freedom, and from freedom in truth comes the capacity to build and plan and act better. Aids in Africa calls us with imperative force to unleash that capacity. **17.04**

Edwin Cameron is a judge of the Supreme Court of Appeal.
This is an edited version of his Edward A Smith Annual Lecture at Harvard Law School's Human Rights Programme

A fight for life over death

Nawaal Deane

"I was not going to vote for this government if my child died of Aids." This was the vow that Nombuyiselo Maphongwane's mother made after witnessing her daughter suffering from full-blown Aids.

Six weeks ago Maphongwane had her will ready. But, having taken anti-retroviral drugs for six weeks, she rediscovered her determination to beat the disease. Her bright eyes and fuller figure are a far cry from the grey-skinned, frail 37-year-old woman waiting for death in April when the *Mail & Guardian* first spoke to her. "It is a miracle how I received these drugs." Her story was published on April 17, the first anniversary of the Cabinet's pledge to provide universal access to anti-retroviral treatment. As a result of the article, Maphongwane received a life-time sponsor for her treatment.

In April her CD4 count was six. The CD4 count determines the strength of the immune system. In June it dropped to four. She did not expect to survive much longer. Six weeks after treatment, her CD4 count has risen to 51. Her weight has increased by about 10kg. Her viral load (used to describe the amount of HIV in the blood) was 350 000 in July and dropped to 281 000 after treatment. Her hair has started growing and her skin has lightened. "I get so excited because I can eat a whole tennis biscuit now," she said.

The miracle began with an article in American magazine *FastCompany*, about Anglo American's HIV/Aids project. Brian Brink, senior vice-president for health, was quoted in the article about the challenges facing South Africans with full-blown Aids who are trying to get treatment. "A lot of people read the article," said Brink. "One person, Alejandro Yarto, was so taken by it that he said he and his family would sponsor treatment for someone in South Africa. They would like to make this commitment of about $1 200 a year — and that they would be able to do this indefinitely."

Yarto said: "We often wonder how we can make an impact on people's lives. What better way to do so than by providing the medicine that makes the difference between life and death?" Brink committed Anglo American to sponsoring the treatment and monitoring of the patient if the drugs were provided. Searching for a candidate, Brink remembered reading about Maphongwane in the *M&G*.

Maphongwane did not hesitate when she heard about the offer. "My family and I were very happy." They had scraped together the money to buy one bottle of Combivir, which she finished in April. "I didn't know where we were going to get the money for more treatment, but we prayed to God." She began treatment on July 14 at Anglo American's clinic. Sister Mamojaki Suping, in charge of the Johannesburg clinic, spoke to her about the possible side effects because of her weakened immune system. "We were all worried," said Suping. "She was very ill ... and I did not think she would survive to even go on the treatment."

Looking at Maphongwane this week it is difficult to remember the frail woman she used to be. Every day she sets her cellphone alarm to remind her to take the tablets, exactly 12 hours apart. "This virus is very clever and if I miss a day of the tablets it learns how to fight the drugs." She has to eat healthy food or she suffers from diarrhoea. "Minister [of Health Manto] Tshabalala-Msimang is right about the nutrition. I don't want to give her credit, but you need healthy food when you are on treatment."

She welcomed the government's announcement that it would provide the drugs. She said the greatest challenge facing the roll-out of anti-retroviral drugs is around stigma: some people will not get the drugs because they do not want to disclose their HIV status. "People [with HIV/Aids] don't want to be identified in Soweto." She said the roll-out will not happen overnight. "The technical team has to set out how these drugs will be dispensed. The health fraternity, activists and communities must work together. We need doctors to monitor the treatment." But Maphongwane warned that the government should not deliberate too long. "Look at the number of young people who have already died of Aids."

Brink said of Maphongwane: "She has been so brave. She has become a leader in showing people that they do not have to fear the treatment." **05.09**

African growth slows

Ferial Haffajee

Zimbabwe emerged as an African laggard last year, its collapsing economy serving to drag continental growth down to 3,2% for 2002, from 4,3% the year before. This emerges from the *Economic Report on Africa 2003* published this week by the Addis Ababa-based Economic Commission for Africa (ECA), a United Nations sub-agency.

The report says that Zimbabwe — once the region's bread-basket — and Liberia raise the spectre of "possible contagious effects in the western and southern sub-regions". The weather and disease also dragged down growth, with droughts in Southern Africa and in the Horn, as well as flooding in North Africa, taking a toll. HIV/Aids is reversing economic gains made in the early 1990s as the disease reaches its killing phase, while tuberculosis and malaria remain maladies that drive down the continent's gross domestic product (GDP) every year.

"The slowdown in regional growth is also due to slower growth in four of the five largest economies in the region: Algeria, Egypt, Morocco and Nigeria," says the report. Conversely, three of Zimbabwe's neighbours — Botswana, Namibia and South Africa — ranked with Mauritius and Tunisia as Africa's star performers, both in terms of their economic management and for putting in place pro-poor policies.

The ECA's economic policy stance index, which ranks each of the 53 countries on the continent, is a method of peer review that will be used by the panelists who next month begin the New Partnership for Africa's Development survey of political and economic governance. Countries are ranked on factors including public budgets, an independent central bank and commercial justice system, a national development plan and a medium-term budget. The ECA also adds points for factors like privatisation and for market liberalisation.

The peer review system sets up a holistic system of measurement. If growth was the sole indicator, the honours would go to Mozambique, which grew 12% in the year under measurement.

Ethiopia, Rwanda and Uganda all grew at more than 6%, but off very low bases. Too many countries are still wild spenders, with budget deficits exceeding 5% of GDP, though the authors say some deficit targets, like those of Mauritius, are being breached for social spending. Countries with double-digit inflation dropped from 30 in 1995 to 11 last year. Zimbabwe's inflation rate of 137,2% was the continent's, and possibly the world's, highest.

What is clear from the annual report, the fourth to be published, is that Africa must increasingly chart its own path and reduce its dependence on aid. The figures are staggering. Mozambique, though the fastest grower, funds 70% of its fiscus from aid; Uganda is 50% aid-dependent, while Rwanda is 60% dependent. "There is mounting evidence that aid in large quantities is a double-edged sword, initially helping but eventually weakening a country's economic performance," the report observes. It adds that only wealthier economies — about one third of the continent — will be able to wean themselves from assistance through a series of economic and social policy measures.

Aid crowds out private investment, a necessary factor for securing the 7% growth rate needed for decent levels of development, according to the report. Foreign direct investment (FDI) also fell by $6-billion between 2001 and the end of 2002 because of a global economic slow-down, but also because of stuttering privatisation. Secondary factors inhibiting investment include the high costs of corruption and weak institutions, which prompt investor concerns that contracts will not be enforced.

While FDI has suffered, the continent has been less buffeted by the September 11 2001 storm and the Iraqi war than anticipated. Rising commodity prices — including those of gold and oil — have given a fillip to producer economies, while tourists have found safe (and cheap) havens on the beaches of Mauritius and in South Africa's game parks.

The report observes that Africa does not sufficiently market the fact that investment on the continent yields the "highest rate of return on investment in the world — four times more than in the G7 countries, twice more than in Asia, and two-thirds more than in Latin America".

Why the fixation with privatisation? The report's authors says that unless non-essential industries are privatised, there is little to invest in on the continent. Two other policy prescriptions hold the key: boosting intra-African trade and raising the continent's percentage of the global tourism market. Unrecorded, and therefore untaxed, cross-border trade accounts for about 30% of Uganda's exports, while almost a quarter of trade in the Economic Community of West African States (Ecowas), is unrecorded. The challenge is to get this trade onto national accounts. Electricity sales in the rest of Africa hold huge potential for the Ugandan and South African economies, says the ECA. "Between 1990 and 2000, tourism in Africa grew at an annual rate of 6,2%, well above the world average of 4,3%."

Peace must come before prosperity, says the ECA. But this is an elusive commodity — by the time the report was in print, its conflict risk-analysis was already outdated. While it punts relative calm in West Africa as part of a string of successful conflict resolutions, Liberia has subsequently been engulfed in bloody civil strife. The Democratic Republic of Congo, potentially an economic powerhouse, is still in the grip of internecine regional conflict. The new conflicts may force the authors to revise their growth predictions for 2003. They suggest growth of 4,2% is achievable.

More countries are expected to benefit from the debt relief programme of the World Bank, the Highly Indebted Poor Countries (HIPC) Initiative, freeing up funds for social spending. In addition, enhanced debt relief should staunch crippling capital flight, which is currently equivalent to sub-Saharan Africa's GDP. Information on 30 countries computed over the 27 years ending in 1996 shows that capital flight amounted to $187-billion, ballooning to $274-billion if interest is taken into account.

As a global economic slump bottoms out and ticks up, Africa will also benefit. And while the aim is still to wean the continent off its post-colonial dependence on donors, for the very poorest countries the promise of increased assistance — amounting to about $12-billion this year — will enhance their contribution to the continent's economy. Better still, says the ECA, would be the dismantling of trade-distorting subsidies by the wealthy countries of the Organisation for Economic Cooperation and Development. "Abolishing OECD agricultural subsidies would provide developing countries with three times their current overseas development assistance [aid] receipts. The elimination of all tariff and non-tariff barriers could result in static gains for developing countries of around $182-billion in services; $162-billion in manufactured goods and $32-billion in agriculture," it comments. **01.08**

'We have no food, no work and no money'

Wisani wa ka Ngobeni

Zimbabwe, as I allowed myself to imagine in the final days before I went there, would be rowdy and in the terrifying grip of a barbaric militia, brandishing long knives. In my imagination there were images of thousands of frail Zimbabweans thronging the city streets and villages. The security forces, I imagined, would be stiffly military, tight-lipped and hostile; anxiously efficient on duty and abandoned when off.

Reality? A week in Zimbabwe reflected what I had envisaged and more: glaring mass poverty, a massive economic crisis and high levels of political intolerance from the ruling party and its security forces. On my arrival last Friday, four foreign journalists, including a reporter for a local daily, were detained by the police. The following week two South African-based journalists were arrested for taking pictures of an empty grain silo. The Zanu-PF militia also stepped up their reign of terror, torturing opposition members at Kuwadzana near Harare ahead of a by-election there.

Working as a journalist in Zimbabwe has become a risky business. The government has enacted new media laws that make it very hard for journalists, especially foreign ones, to cover the ongoing crisis in that country. The laws require local journalists and newspapers to get an annually renewable "licence", at the discretion of the government. Foreign journalists are required to get accreditation before they leave their home countries. Journalists without accreditation risk being arrested and deported. Although I was a bit concerned about the consequences, I did not try to get the accreditation as it would have been a futile exercise.

Last year Zimbabwe Information and Publicity Minister Jonathan Moyo warned that "elements [journalists] who sneak into the country without accreditation are operating illegally. If caught they might take a long time to go back to their home country," he said.

Despite my initial qualms I agreed to go. My first stop was Harare, the capital. The plan was to spend three days there before I dashed off to Bulawayo. I landed at Harare International airport with a scrap of paper in my pocket. On the paper was the name of a person I was supposedly visiting and his address. After a short interrogation at the checkpoint the immigration officer allowed me in. It was about 8pm. The lights in the airport foyer did not provide much brightness, but one could still see a string of portraits of President Robert Mugabe hung on almost every wall in the airport building.

At the hotel a picture of Mugabe was hammered into the brickwork in the reception area. Almost every hotel and public institution has one or two photos of the 78-year-old president in black suit and large spectacles. I had witnessed this phenomenon in Kenya last year. I wonder what the new Kenyan government has decided to do with former president Daniel arap Moi's portraits, which were also a common sight in private and public buildings. The reader must excuse me for not doing my research on that one.

On my first day in Harare I woke up at 6am. By 7am I was on the streets. It was a wet and grey Saturday morning. A light drizzle was falling like confetti, melting into the empty pavements. There were few signs of life, just the occasional shriek of taxis and the blistering shunt of buses driving in and out of the city centre. Each sound echoed briefly, then was swallowed by the silence. Some shops on Samora Machel Road were open, but there was nobody much about.

Harare is a drab city. It has a population of 1,6-million. The people here rise each day with a glare on their face and run out to the city, determined to succeed. In the city centre, where not many of the buildings — except the high-rise office blocks along the main streets — have seen fresh paint in the past decade, they stand in queues for the better part of the day. There are mealiemeal queues, bread queues, cooking oil queues, salt queues and sugar queues. Some streets in the inner city are forever deserted. All one sees are parked cars (cars spend more time parked than on the road because of chronic fuel shortages) and random bits of rubbish blown in by the wind. Most people I spoke to said life in Zimbabwe is a lot harder than it was a year or two ago. The collapse of the commercial farming sector has left tens of thousands of people destitute.

One of those people is Abraham Banda (46). Banda used to work on a tobacco farm outside Harare before the white farmer was forced off the land. With no prospect of employment in the countryside, Banda, like many other people who once worked on commercial farms, has drifted to Harare. He shares a single-bedroom flat with seven other people. He arrived in Harare eight months ago with the hope of finding a job. He has not found a position yet.

Banda said he relies on food aid to survive. Every morning, along with hordes of visibly frail Zimbabweans, he goes to various churches in Harare hoping to get a meal. He often does not get one. "Sometimes I have spent more than three days without food. I am really suffering. I hope the government can do something about this problem," he said, adding that he had once collapsed from hunger while queuing for food. "I pray every day that someone out there gives me food. People I know have died in the villages because of lack of food. I wish that I will not have to die due to hunger."

A Harare resident said the level of desperation among the people is very high. "The food situation here is very worrying indeed, and it is happening in a country that was once the bread-basket of Southern Africa," he said.

A recent case, in which a man married off his 10-year-old daughter, despite her protests and threats to commit suicide, to a 58-year-old friend in return for mealiemeal paints a stark picture of the level of desperation. The bridegroom was convicted last week of rape of a minor. The girl's father died in a prison cell. Locals say such cases have become common in the country as the economic crisis continues to bite. Stories of people eating worms and grass have been common in the local media in the recent past.

Last week Zimbabwean retail shop owners complained that poverty has led to a massive increase in shoplifting. People are committing one offence after another. More than 20 new cases of shoplifting are recorded at most courts each day. Most cases reported involve theft of basic commodities such as soap, cooking oil, sugar, clothing and even building materials.

In Maphisa, about 100km outside Bulawayo, residents complained that they are forced to eat caterpillars and maggots because of the food shortage. "We have no food, no work and no money. How are we supposed to feed our families now?" asked Mathews Sibanda. "If you walk around here, you will see that the stomachs of children are growing bigger and swollen by malnutrition. People are starving here. It is not unusual here for a person to spend more than four days without food. Children are often given one meal a day," the 50-year-old said.

The food crisis has affected attendance at the local school. A teacher at Minda Primary School said some classes that used to have 100 pupils now have half that number. Sibanda blamed politicians for the problems in his area. He should know: he is a former Zanu-PF councillor for Maphisa. He was fired from Zanu-PF at the end of his term last year for cooperating with the opposition in his area.

Maphisa is one of the 24 wards in the Matobo District. The governor of Matobo is Stephen Nkomo, younger brother of the late Zimbabwean vice-president Joshua Nkomo. Stephen Nkomo is ill and has been in hospital for the past three weeks. Mugabe visited him last week, while in Bulawayo for a meeting with more than 200 traditional leaders. At the meeting Mugabe promised to give each traditional leader a car. "I guess it will not be difficult to buy 266 cars for our chiefs," the president said. It is not the first time Zimbabwe's chiefs have benefited from Mugabe's regime. They were recently awarded allowances of Z$50 000 (about R6 250) a month. In addition to the cars, the chiefs will soon receive cellphones and homes with an electricity supply. Yet the same chiefs are often accused of worsening the conditions of the rural poor.

Last week a Zimbabwean daily newspaper carried a front-page headline: "Chief sells maize as the villagers starve". The daily claimed that food aid aimed at villagers was being sold by the chief on the black market. The chief apparently sold a 10-litre bucket of mealiemeal for Z$5 000. After the meeting with Mugabe the chiefs pleaded with him not to retire before the end of his term. "Stepping down now will be a betrayal of the people," they said.

People in Maphisa disagree with the chiefs' stance. They believe

Zanu-PF has failed to rule the country. The hopes and aspirations that political independence promised have been shattered by Mugabe's misrule, they say. They also slate Nkomo for failing to rise above the challenges facing his district.

Nkomo is not only a politician, he is also a businessman. He owns the only petrol station in the Matobo District. When I visited the area, Nkomo's petrol station was deserted. An old car battery was pushed neatly out of the way against a wall. There was little traffic on the road alongside the petrol station and, like so many other tiny roads snaking nearby, it led nowhere.

The road from Bulawayo to Maphisa was a marvel — it is so narrow it can only accommodate a single car. There are signs every 10km warning "deadly hazard". The tarmac has been worn away in places, revealing the grey cobblestones of the road underneath. It is not worth repairing.

Residents said Nkomo's petrol station has been without fuel for about seven days. Yet they were quick to point out that the fuel crisis was not a major concern to them. "People are unemployed and hungry. Every day they scavenge in the nearby woods for roots and fruit. People eat almost anything here, including worms," Sibanda said. He added that food distribution to his area has been hampered by political infighting. "We often get food aid, but the distribution is inconsistent. Some people are also excluded from food aid because of their political affiliation," he said.

Sibanda said HIV/Aids worsened the situation in his area. "We have an HIV/Aids council in the area. The council is supposed to organise food and clothes for people affected by the disease. But political differences have hindered that process. None of the 24 wards in Matobo have submitted their programmes to the district Aids coordinator. "According to statistics about 200 people are dying of Aids every month and we have 400 to 500 new infections every month. Besides that, we have orphans who are no longer attending school. There is a fund which is supposed to support them, but it is not," he said.

Sibanda said the people in his area also do not have access to proper health care. "The Maphisa Central hospital has collapsed. There are no drugs in the hospital, but you have to pay about Z$120 to be treated. People do not have any money to go to hospital. A lot of them die at their homes as they cannot afford to go to hospital."

Although a local mining operation in the area was providing jobs for the people, the majority is still unemployed, he said. The acute shortage of fuel and the lack of foreign currency have led to a massive industrial crunch. It has also led to a massive boom of the so-called black market, which runs a parallel foreign exchange service.

At the centre of it all is Zimbabwe's skewed exchange rate system. The Zimbabwean dollar's official rate to the United States dollar stands at Z$55 to US$1. The official exchange rates for the British pound and South African rand, are Z$75, and Z$8 respectively. On the black market the US dollar trades at Z$1 500, the British pound fetches Z$2 200, and the rand sells at Z$150.

In Bulawayo locals have nicknamed Fort Street, where the black market operates, the "World Bank of Zimbabwe". Women operate the "bank". They sit all day on the pavements waiting for customers. Most of them carry more than Z$1-million (R125 000) at a time. The only acceptable foreign currencies are the US dollar, British pound and the South African rand. Undercover police patrol the pavements, but they have failed to curb the activity. The black-market supplies businesses with foreign currency, which they use to import goods. In addition to providing a foreign exchange service, they also sell rare commodities such as mealiemeal and sugar. They also sell petrol and paraffin. The black-market prices are, however, beyond the reach of millions of Zimbabweans. Petrol costs Z$1 000 a litre on the black market, while the official price is Z$74,47.

The price of petrol was last reviewed in 1999 despite movement in the price of crude oil, the steep decline of the Zimbabwean dollar against hard currencies and escalating inflation. One car dealer in Harare had the following to say about the situation: "If you want to go by the formal sector and the official exchange rates in Zimbabwe, you will be out of business within minutes, if not seconds. The government's price controls on foodstuffs mean that companies are forced to operate at a loss and eventually they are also forced out of business. The problem is that Zimbabwe's exchange rate system is so distorted that for those who are forced to follow it they find themselves failing to sustain their business operations," the dealer said.

The massive economic crisis is easy to notice. Industrial areas in Harare and Bulawayo resemble ghost towns as many companies have closed shop, shedding hundreds of jobs. In both cities most supermarket shelves are empty, but massive queues can still be found throughout the day. The people disperse only when the shops close for the day. "You cannot leave the queue because you do not know when food will arrive. If you move, you will miss out," one woman said.

With inflation running at 198%, the incomes of the few who are still lucky enough to hold on to their jobs have been severely eroded. An average worker earns between $20 000 and $30 000, but has to spend about $500 on transport daily ($15 000 a month). In addition, people have to cope with a transport system that has collapsed as a result of fuel shortages. Daily a steady stream of people can be seen walking and cycling along the road during rush hour in both Harare and Bulawayo. A number of them say they are tired of waiting long hours for buses, others say they simply cannot afford the exorbitant fares.

Many people say they are forced to walk more than 40km a day to get to work because buses do not always show up. Fuel woes have also hit cross-border transport operators, who are forced to charge customers higher prices in order to sustain their businesses. A trip from Harare to Johannesburg costs between Z$16 000 and Z$30 000.

Accommodation is also extremely expensive. Rent in the inner city starts from about Z$10 000, while in the suburbs the minimum rental for a single room is between Z$3 000 and Z$4 000. These prices exclude water and electricity. Houses for sale in the suburbs fetch between Z$20-million and $40-million. An old 1986 Mazda 323 will set you back between Z$3-million and Z$5-million and a decent meal for four people at a restaurant costs more than Z$4 000, without drinks. A chicken burger, without chips, at a restaurant fetches about Z$1 600; a mixed grill at a Spur about Z$6 000 and a can of Coke about Z$500. A cup of coffee in Zimbabwe costs Z$400.

The United Nations's latest report on the humanitarian situation in Zimbabwe shows that 62% of the country's population will be in need of food aid by March. This means that 7,2-million people in Zimbabwe will go hungry, an increase from the 6,7-million already surviving on food handouts.

But one thing that *is* easy to find is beer. A Bulawayo resident told me if beer supplies run dry, maybe ordinary Zimbabweans will know the economy has collapsed. He said it appears that in the past few years of political chaos and economic decline, the brewing industry has become the heart of the Zimbabwean economy.

It is a convincing claim. In almost every village, even the remotest, the liquor stores were stocked. Even though food is not reaching villages, beer is. Natisa Village, about 60km outside Bulawayo, has three liquor stores and one food store in one small shopping complex. Poor people in rural Zimbabwe drink traditional beer called Ndovu. A litre of Ndovu cost about Z$300. In the city centre, most Zimbabweans reach for Castle and Lion. Although the country has its own beer, Zambezi, most people prefer Lion. "As I do not have a lot of money to spend on alcohol I always buy Lion, because I get drunk faster. Lion has the highest alcohol volume compared with the other beers," said one man in a pub in Bulawayo. The prices of beer vary depending on where you buy it. The liquor-store price is normally about Z$250 for a 400ml beer, while at a restaurant in the city centre it cost about Z$450.

What is astonishing in both Harare and Bulawayo was the deep hush that descended after 10pm — a far cry from the vibe that used to exist in these towns. Although nightclubs in both cities attract large numbers of people at night, you don't see them roaming the streets. It was almost spine-chilling. Maybe the fact that the price of drinks in some bars and nightclubs doubles after 10pm has something to do with it. Or maybe it was the entrance fee of between $500 and $1 000. Or maybe it is the appalling condition of many clubs in the inner city. At one club I went to in Bulawayo the lighting was so subdued that it took me a full 10 minutes before my eyes became accustomed to the smoky gloom.

The music at the club was South African. South Africa's Mzekezeke is a hot favourite and gets ample airplay on the state-controlled radio stations. But airplay does not translate to massive sales in Zimbabwe. It is not that Zimbabweans do not want to buy CDs. They cannot afford it; a CD costs about Z$14 000 (R1 750), or more.

Njabulo Ncube, a senior journalist with the *Financial Gazette* in Zimbabwe, told me at the end of my trip: "Zimbabwe used to be a nice place. We used to enjoy ourselves here. Now it is very bad. I am working here but I will never be able to afford a car. Where will I get Z$5-million?" The trick is, Ncube said, to think less or not to think at all about cars, CDs and other luxuries. After all, one can live without CDs. **07.02**

LETTER

Drought of good governance

The situation in Zimbabwe can be described by Nigerian novelist Chinua Achebe's statement in his book, *The Trouble with Nigeria*. Achebe says: "The trouble with Nigeria is simply and squarely a failure of leadership. There is nothing basically wrong with the Nigerian character. There is nothing wrong with the Nigerian land or climate or water or air, or anything else. The Nigerian problem is the unwillingness or inability of its leaders to rise to the responsibility, to the challenge of personal example, which is the hallmark of true leadership."

People should not waste time debating the causes of hunger and economic collapse in Zimbabwe because it is clear that the government has failed. Twenty-two years in power is enough to make a positive change. The only change Zanu-PF has made is destroying the economy. The drought cannot be blamed for everything. What about the fuel shortage — is that the drought as well? In 1992 we had one of the worst droughts, but we never ran out of sugar, mealie meal, bread, soft drinks, salt and even the most basic things like toilet paper.

Surely our dear old president should be man enough and step down? Saying the shortages are caused by Britain's interference is total rubbish. Britain never invaded any farm, nor did it tell the oil company not to pay its debts. Britain has no war veterans who disrupt farming and the distribution of food.

The bottom line is that the corrupt, illegitimate Zanu-PF government has ruined the country and the people must do something now. The truth is that in Zimbabwe there is a drought of good governance and the ability to rule. To the African leaders who always defend President Robert Mugabe: One day justice will prevail. — *Zenzele Ndebele, Bulawayo, 24.01*

"I'm not exactly sure why Zimbabweans are flooding to South Africa." — Minister of Labour Membathisi Mdladlana, on talks with his Zimbabwean counterpart, July Moyo, about migrant workers and illegal immigrants 10.01

The unstoppable tide

Sean O'Toole

"I'm tired of this," remarked a South African National Defence Force (SANDF) soldier offloading a small group of glum-looking immigrants at the Musina police station, a ramshackle collection of squat buildings in South Africa's most northerly outpost. It was not yet mid-morning and the soldier's company had arrested yet another batch of desperate Zimbabweans illegally crossing the nearby Limpopo river. "Night and day, all the time, every day the same," he sighed, leading the men to the station's cells.

"I haven't eaten for two days," said 24-year-old Phillip Chikumbo, his dark eyes bloodshot with fatigue. There was no hint of outrage or bitterness in his comment; he was simply hungry. "They do not have food for us here because we are unexpected visitors."

Dressed in a blue-and-white check shirt, his hair closely cropped, Chikumbo is one of about 20 young men — all Zimbabwean — patiently awaiting deportation to a place he no longer wants to call home. "My father is not very happy," he said, squatting on his haunches among a tangle of roots belonging to a wild fig that prospered in the middle of the prison courtyard. "He is angry that I left; he says it's running away. But there is nothing to do [in Zimbabwe] as far as a job. It's hard to raise money."

A qualified mechanic, Chikumbo was born and raised in Chiredzi, in Zimbabwe's central Mashonaland district. Long disheartened by the lack of opportunity in the country, he is an old hand at crossing the border illegally. Chikumbo works as a junior mechanic at a private trucking company on the road to Thohoyandou. It is not an uncommon story told in the prison courtyard. Maxwell (33), "caught in an ambush along the river", has been a mall security guard in Johannesburg for nine years. Morris (18), from Masvingo, earns R750 as a tractor driver on a Mpumalanga farm.

"I get paid R600 a month," said Chikumbo. Exploitation wages to be sure, but he is happy with the opportunity to work. The income allows him to visit his girlfriend Sara every three to four months in Chiredzi. Chikumbo said his arrest is a minor inconvenience, his words echoing the sentiments of many of the detainees. Take, for example, Freedom Kulalelo (23). Arrested two weeks ago in the Johannesburg suburb of Berea, he spent 10 days at Lindela repatriation centre near Krugersdorp. After his return to Zimbabwe he headed straight back to South Africa.

It used to be, a policeman told us, that Zimbabweans detained illegally crossing into South Africa were fined upon repatriation. They were even sent away to Harare. But occurrences of illegal crossings are so frequent along this border (26 742 in 2000, 19 932 in 2001, and 18 033 recorded last year) that the Zimbabwean authorities have stopped imposing punitive sanctions. At worst, one border-jumper told us, they might be told to clean the Beit Bridge police station before being released.

"I have been disturbed from my programme," commented Maxwell, who had been following our conversation intently. Tinged with a suggestion of humour, Maxwell's comment nonetheless articulated the thoughts of many of those in the Musina prison. "I am late for work now," he quipped, adding: "It's very obvious. I can't live in that place of [President Robert] Mugabe anymore. I'm coming back — today." Chikumbo smiled: "Me too."

We arranged to meet Chikumbo in Beit Bridge with the aim of accompanying him on his illegal border crossing. Having previously visited this Zimbabwean town perched on the periphery of Mugabe's politically besieged country, we knew it to be relatively docile, which is not to say it is a benign, sleepy hollow. Stern Zanu-PF banners in the town's centre offered a reminder of the larger context: "Land Reform for Economic Empowerment," one of them read.

A necessary pit stop for migrants travelling south, the town of Beit Bridge presents many obstacles. Aside from the obdurate plainclothes policeman from the criminal investigations department, there are also exploitative taxi drivers, dissolute gangs of robbers (otherwise known as the *guma guma*), rapacious crocodiles and the SANDF.

"You have to be clever," Kulalelo told us, particularly when it comes to the *guma guma*. "They don't have guns, but they carry spears, screwdrivers, axes, knives." While crossing the Limpopo, Kulalelo saw a woman being raped by eight of them, an allegation later confirmed by a SANDF patrol.

By all accounts the *guma guma* are motivated by economic expediency alone, a fact emphasised by the Shona meaning of the word. Loosely translated, *guma guma* means to get something by no effort. One migrant we spoke to said the word was actually onomatopoeic, deriving from the sound of pigs eating. This aptly pegs the *guma guma* for what they are, scavengers who prey on naive, often cash-rich border-jumpers.

Operating in bandit groups along the Beit Bridge border area, the guma guma ostensibly offer guided walks and/or taxi journeys to various points along the South Africa/Zimbabwe border. They charge a minimum of R50 for leading migrants to purpose-cut holes in the South African border fence, a 180km tangle of electric wires delineating the political boundary between the two countries.

Chikumbo's protracted ritual breaching of this patchwork fence, a toothless beast that is a throwback to apartheid times, merely highlights the ease with which border-jumpers cross the border with impunity. With the cost of processing undocumented migrants said to be R16 000 a person, the implications of these crossings are by no means inconsequential. Last year the SANDF arrested 50 852 immigrants along South Africa's borders with Zimbabwe, Mozambique, Swaziland and Botswana.

After being offloaded by a Department of Home Affairs truck at the Beit Bridge police station Chikumbo immediately headed for the township of Dulibadzimo, on the outskirts of town. At the central market he chartered a sky-blue Datsun taxi, at a cost of Z$35 000 (R90). "It's not a good business," the lanky taxi-driver confided as he drove us an hour or so east of Beit Bridge. "Fuel is too expensive."

The scenery on our drive was revealing. Drought and profligate overgrazing have destroyed the landscape. Only the baobabs prosper. We passed four men walking. Chikumbo waved. "They were with me in prison this morning," he chuckled. "They're also going back."

The taxi ride came to an end at a dusty soccer field 20km east of Beit Bridge. From there we had to walk, the mass of small rural paths finally congregating into one well-worn (smuggler's) path that led us to the river. I asked Chikumbo about the crocodiles, which have been known to take migrants. "It's a matter of starvation," he said. "You can't worry about those things."

We eventually forded the Limpopo by moonlight, darting around slimy pools of stagnant water. When there was no way around these, we waded knee-deep through the river. On the South African side a bedraggled series of farm fences hinted that we were not the first visitors to crawl under the first, then hop over the second.

It is really that simple gaining entry into South Africa, though the reality for many border-jumpers is that they will be detained by the SANDF in Musina. But this is nothing compared with the disastrous situation in Zimbabwe. "It's true! It's real!" said Chikumbo. "People from the opposition are being killed; even job applications are turned down. People are angry."

As long as this anger is unattended to, it seems that Musina's prison courtyard will continue to be a congregation point for the youths who gather there like the collected flotsam of some invisible shipwreck: Zimbabwe. **03.10**

One year after Savimbi

Justin Pearce

If you want to know what is going on in Angola, Luanda airport is always a good place to start. At the military end, the Antonovs now sit idle for days on end. A year ago the apron would be clear by 8am, after the lumbering Russian planes set off for the towns of the interior. They carried soldiers and military hardware, but also beer, cooking oil, radio batteries, soap.

Those were the days when Unita still roamed freely through most of the countryside, so what little internal trade there was in Angola took place by air, and it was the Angolan army generals who reaped the profits. Today the roads are still full of potholes and there has been an alarming number of anti-tank mine incidents — but that has not stopped the generals from switching to the road-haulage business, using military trucks, and putting the Antonovs out to pasture.

At the international passenger terminal there are more Boeings than before — in November, British Airways became the latest big carrier to open a route to Luanda, with more foreigners arriving to get their slice of Angola's ever-expanding petroleum industry. And the Hercules transport planes operated by the World Food Programme are busier than ever.

During the last months of the war, the Angolan Armed Forces (FAA) moved thousands of people off their land in an attempt to isolate Unita, which itself survived on looting and raiding. By the end of the war, 1,5-million people were living on humanitarian aid. That figure has risen to two million since the war ended, but the statistic masks the reality that things are getting better. More people have managed to get access to emergency food, and the first post-war harvest is due soon.

To try and make sense of all this, you could look to the oddly-shaped little single-propeller plane, painted in military camouflage, parked near to where men are loading grain sacks on to the Hercules. "That's the plane that killed Jonas Savimbi," said a Angolan journalist.

The Brazilian-made Toucano reconnaissance plane was used to track down the Unita rebel leader until he was cornered and shot dead on February 22 last year. The remaining leadership agreed to talks, and the result was a formal ceasefire signed on April 4. The FAA continues to battle separatist rebels in Cabinda, but the other 17 Angolan provinces have been at peace since then.

But was Savimbi's death really a necessary condition for ending the war? It has since become evident that Unita's founder was ready to enter peace talks at least two months before he was killed. Back then, churches and civilian peace activists had been hoping that a ceasefire would lead to a broad dialogue on Angola's future, which would have extended the debate beyond the government and Unita.

By killing Savimbi before the talks could happen, the government grabbed the political initiative. Unita's half-starved generals happily talked on the government's terms, and the dialogue that did take place was all about the technicalities of disarming Unita's army in fulfilment of the 1994 Lusaka accord. Adrift without its autocratic founder, Unita gained few concessions other than a year's worth of luxury hotel accommodation for its leaders, and vastly ambitious promises of assistance for its rank-and-file soldiers.

Angolans outside of the two main gun-toting political camps continued to demand a say in the process; all that happened was that a handful of organisations were invited to put their views to the United Nations after the real decisions had been made.

The passing of Savimbi may not have been a precondition for peace, but it certainly determined what shape that peace took. One European diplomat put it bluntly: "If you remember, the war was a matter of two elites screwing the Angolan people. Well, now peace is a matter of two elites screwing the Angolan people."

Yet no one denies that a two-party system is better than a de facto one-party system. The smaller parties that emerged after the official adoption of multiparty democracy in 1992 have done little to loosen the MPLA's grip on the resources of the state. This is why several foreign governments are now giving their support, be it tacit or overt, to Unita as it seeks to rebrand itself as a civilian opposition party.

Can Unita do that? It was Savimbi's portrait that stared down at the British and American ambassadors as they sat as front-row observers at a recent meeting of Unita's political commission, yet the new leadership is doing its best to distance itself from the absolutist legacy of *O mais velho* (the elder), Savimbi. When the Angolan media leapt on to rumours of party in-fighting, Unita officials were equally quick to spin this as a symptom of healthy democratic debate.

Being an opposition party in Angola ought not to be difficult. The country of 13-million people earns about $10-billion, most of it from oil, each year, yet still managed to rank number 161 on a scale of 173 countries assessed in the UN's Human Development Report last year.

About the same time, a leaked International Monetary Fund report gave a clue to the nature of the problem, revealing that $4-billion had vanished from state revenues in five years. The fact that the MPLA is still tipped to walk through the next election (which always seems to be two years in the future, and is now predicted for 2005) is a sign of how deeply dug-in the party is, rather than an endorsement of its recent performance in the government.

Getting 100 000 former Unita guerrillas resettled and in gainful employment may not be the only thing the government has to do at the moment. But it is generally seen as the most urgent, given that many of the soldiers are believed to have hung on to their weapons during a demobilisation process that was never properly audited.

But if the disarmament drive was flawed, resettlement plans have gone nowhere at all. The provision of "resettlement kits" — farming tools, seeds and other essentials of life — to Unita's men was held up for six months after the contract to do this was awarded to a company owned by a close associate of President José Eduardo dos Santos. Things look better where the resettlement of displaced civilians is concerned — 1,3-million have returned home since the end of the war — but most of them did so on their own initiative with no government or foreign assistance. Many are going to areas that are still infested with landmines, and where it will take at least another year to become self-sufficient in food.

One UN official insisted that there are plenty of people in the government who want to get things done. Unfortunately, those are not the same people who have the cash at their disposal to do so, since funds get tied up at the level of the presidency — known as *futungo* after the seaside suburb that houses the presidential compound. "As long as *futungo* is there, the problem remains. And *futungo* is not just going to go away. So we have to work with what there is," the official said.

There are indeed other signs that the government can deliver when it chooses to. Since Savimbi died, "normalisation" has become the order of the day. The remnants of war are a mess unbecoming a country that now holds the presidency of the Southern African Development Community (SADC) and a seat on the UN Security Council. So there were plans to close the displaced people's camps and Unita quartering areas by October 2002; those plans were put on hold after Unita and aid agencies pointed out that there was nowhere else for people to go.

Closer to home, in Luanda, the government has had more success in its cosmetic efforts. Pretty public squares with lawns and fountains have been popping up all over the city centre, while the *bairros* (townships) remain without running water, electricity or sewerage. People who have no taps in their homes will sometimes help themselves from the lawn sprinklers in the parks, provided they can dodge the security guards.

The SADC summit in Luanda in October saw a new frenzy of painting, and squadrons of street sweepers were deployed throughout the city centre after dark. But the government's zeal when it comes to cleaning up downtown doesn't stop at litter.

In a city where the sole family breadwinner is often a woman who makes a few dollars a day selling fruit or vegetables on the street, the authorities have launched a new fiscal police force with the express task of chasing the vendors away, fining them and confiscating their goods. And in a city where housing shortages have driven people to live in drains or ruined buildings, the provincial authorities in December demolished 1 000 solid, new owner-occupied houses in the Soba Kapassa neighbourhood. Residents are still wondering why. "They forget they were elected to run the country, and they do things that are just not right," said one man who had supported the MPLA until the bulldozers moved in.

Such mutterings of discontent are growing, in a country where the very idea of dissent still causes consternation. Last month an independent newspaper published a list of Angola's richest people. It was the kind of thing that anywhere else would have been dismissed as a light weekend feature, but in Angola it sparked a debate that dominated the media for weeks afterwards — possibly because of the disproportionate number of ruling party officials who made it on to the list. The formerly socialist MPLA put out a statement saying that such criticism was unpatriotic. As one Angolan journalist put it, "the workers' party has become the millionaires' party".

Ask Angolans why they are so reluctant to complain publicly about their lot and you will get one of two answers. Some will recall the government's violent response to an attempted coup in 1977, when thousands of suspected dissidents were slaughtered; others say that decades of war have lowered expectations, even bred fatalism. But most Angolans were born after 1977, and the war is now over.

The northern Angola town of Uige still bears bullet scars, but its market is booming. This is due largely to the retirement of the Antonovs in favour of more economical road transport to get the goods in. It is a modest boom admittedly — not everyone can afford a whole tin of tomato paste, so the women will sell you half a tin, with clingwrap over the open end — but there are many more products and many more stalls than before.

Recently, when a policeman started interfering with the traders, people threw stones at him. When his commanding officer tried to intervene, he too was chased away. Said one resident of the town: "That would never have happened a year ago." **21.02**

Tears of rage

Shaun de Waal

The new Bruce Willis vehicle, *Tears of the Sun,* is so bad and so offensive that it doesn't deserve a review. Then again, having sat through it, the least I can do to make myself feel better is use this space to denounce it. Perhaps I'm a little ratty because I had, just before seeing it, been subjected to *Anger Management*. And just as I was recovering from *Tears of the Sun* I was assaulted by *The Hunted*.

Tears of the Sun is set in Africa — Nigeria, to be precise. One can be precise because the movie is prefaced by fake TV footage telling us that there's a civil war on in Nigeria: "this once-peaceful country" (I'm choking) is at war; "the majority of Ibo have abandoned their homes", and so on. The US embassy and other foreign nationals are being evacuated. That's precise enough, though which Nigerian civil war is being referred to is unclear — not the Biafran one, I don't think, because the military hardware we see a bit later seems too contemporary. Perhaps it's a new one that's just broken out in darkest Africa, which, as we know, is a constant rumble of civil wars, high-, low- or medium-level. The fact that Africa really is so troubled is of course annoying to anyone trying not to be an "Afro-pessimist", but what's going on in *Tears of the Sun* does not engage with reality in any meaningful way. Africa is a fictional space for most Americans, so anything they like can be projected on to it.

The fake TV footage having set the scene, there is a surge of important music and we're "somewhere off the coast of Africa", or so a subtitle informs us. We're on a US army aircraft carrier, and Bruce Willis and men have just arrived back from rescuing some US citizens from the rampant natives. They're all grubby and have the odd attractively placed minor wounds. They are looking forward to their bunks and their chow. But barely have they got out of their copter than tough commander Tom Skerrit, who's had a lot of practice playing tough commanders, is telling them they have to go back almost at once to rescue a woman doctor working in a remote mission hospital. Would it have been so urgent had the doctor been male? One suspects not.

At any rate, the doctor is indeed female, and beautiful too, because she is played by Monica Bellucci. Monica is Italian, naturally, but (as the commander explains for the sake of viewers wondering why they cast her) she is an American citizen and thus she must be rescued at once. We're also told by the commander that her husband is dead, so we (and Bruce) know she's single. It's called dramatic tension. After some chummy macho briefing stuff with the tough commander, Bruce et al are off again in their helicopters.

Bruce has not yet required the use of his facial muscles, but soon he will. Monica doesn't want to be rescued unless the people she's been helping can come too. Bruce has his orders, but he's willing to try to trick her into leaving the mission. He agrees to take Monica *and* her Africans. The "rebels" are approaching. Cue wantonly manipulative and very tearful farewell from the European missionaries at the hospital. They will stay to be massacred. In the meantime, Bruce will schlepp Monica and her Africans through the jungle, with a narrow escape or two, to the rendezvous point, and then he'll kidnap Monica and abandon the Africans. So far so good.

Except that as they fly away, and Monica gets all tearful, Bruce has a spasm of facial movement and decides they've got to go back. They've got to get as many Africans as possible on to the helicopter, then Bruce and his faithful band of men will take Monica and the rest of them through the jungle and across the border to Cameroon. He is, of course, disobeying orders. The audience is deeply impressed. The façade of Bruce's brute bald manliness has been ripped away to reveal the sensitive human being beneath. In the meantime, the rebels have arrived at the mission station and massacred everyone. The rebels are, after all, led by two evil-looking commanders, one who barks orders in a savage way and one who tends to just smirk evilly from behind his dark glasses.

Bruce, Monica, et al tramp through the jungle, chased by the evil rebels. A variety of predictable set-pieces and hoary old clichés come to pass, including the scene of soldierly camaraderie in which Bruce asks his men if they're with him or against him. Then there's a particularly nauseating scene when they come across a village being ravaged by the rebels, with some grotesque brutality thrown in, which is all very upsetting until you realise it's not there to do anything except justify the summary justice promptly meted out by Bruce and his men, and to provide the filmmakers with a bit of shoot-'em-up action.

And so we trudge on toward the Cameroonian border. There's lots of gooey music, and the moments of tension and fear are relieved by passages of sentimentality. For instance, there's an attractively headscarved African woman who keeps trembling on the verge of tears, asking the black American solider (there had to be one) to assure her everything will be alright. She keeps trembling on the brink of tears until Bruce has effected the final rescue, when she finally spills over and commends him, in religiose broken English, for his wonderful work on behalf of the continent. This is the point at which the viewer is torn between the urge to laugh and the desire to vomit. If only everyone in the Third World were as weepily grateful for everything the United States has done for them.

What is worse than sentimentality, that great besetting sin of popular art? I'll tell you: American military macho sentimentality is worse. The solemnity with which Bruce conducts himself through all this balderdash is there to tell you that this is a serious movie, not just popular entertainment. Except he's lying — it is popular entertainment of the most expensive, indulgent and idiot-brained kind. The clichés of darkest Africa are recycled, not to make us think about some of the terrible things that happen in Africa (that is Nepad's job, isn't it?), but to provide a setting in which Bruce Willis can perform heroic feats on behalf of the benighted natives.

Either *Tears of the Sun* is appallingly naive or it is disgustingly cynical. It's hard not to go with the latter: this saga of the US saving Africa from itself can only be seen in the context of the US saving Iraq from itself, although that adventure seems to have been marginally less successful in the long run than Bruce Willis's efforts in Nigeria. He should be sent to Iraq immediately. **20.06**

LETTER: IN BRIEF

After observing President Thabo Mbeki's leadership on Aids, Zimbabwe, concentrating power in the president's office, loyalty to cronies, and now on the Nigerian election, it is clear what Nepad stands for: Not Exactly Proposing Anything Different. — *Richard Owen, Harare, 02.05*

Home is where the hurt is

Matthew Krouse

The National Arts Festival is an exercise in tolerance — tolerance of Grahamstown's new parking meter system, for example. The local press has called it a "parking war". What it boils down to is the use of car guards as mobile meters.

When one alights from one's vehicle a bibbed guard keys one's registration number into a hand-held computer. When one returns, the same individual pockets one's cash. Up until the start of the festival on June 27 there was conflict between the authorities and residents about parking rates and the geographical extent of the new deal. Just hours ahead of the festival's opening, the issue was resolved. And so it took off, this employment plan initiated by the local Makana council with an empowerment firm called Diversified Parking Systems.

As Grahamstown grumbled through its new street law, the artists and audiences pulled in. In front of the quaint Victorian façades stalls popped up. Over the festival's 29 years, the appropriateness of this town as a location for this cultural event of national importance has been hotly debated. In fact, the issue of whether Grahamstown's annual jamboree embodies a national culture has come under scrutiny time and again. Now some new turns have inched this discussion closer to being resolved.

The idea of a national arts festival would of necessity have to include a notion of nationhood. And nationhood, by its very definition, has to include a sense of belonging. Arriving for the festival one invariably wonders just how all-inclusive the experience is going to be. The level of sponsorship obviously says something about marketers' perceptions of such an event. If the public is buying into an idea, you can be sure powerful brand names are too. This year — the second since Standard Bank pulled back as sole sponsor — the event is fully endorsed, even though it has not been by the guardians of style. There's the Lottery, the SABC, the Eastern Cape government, the National Arts Council and the scaled-down involvement of Standard Bank. And so this new set presides (in tandem with the festival committee), almost as tolerant parents, over the nation's ideas.

Meanwhile, the children play and play. And play. And as we've learnt from the Bard: play is a mirror of life.

If the 2003 edition of the National Arts Festival has been about anything, it has been a grand-scale meditation on the subject of home. The notion of home has hovered as a symbolic catch-all above so many cultural products that it's almost cause for alarm. Or rather, cause for celebration. That's if one understands that by interrogating home, artists are turning away from having to deal prescriptively with themes like race, democracy and reconciliation and beginning to look deeper within.

The main platform for this exploration has been the festival exhibition *Homing in*, curated by Durban's Virginia MacKenny and Cape Town's Paul Edmunds. They present installations by eight emerging artists whose work deals with the South African home as "a contested site of meaning". This space, they note in their catalogue, is "dominated by a colonial heritage, disrupted by migrant labour and historically problematised by the old regime's creation of homelands". As South Africans, they write, we are "searching for a place one might legitimately call home".

Sparse as it is, *Homing in* presents an object-laden vision of a place of disorientation. In a white room Durban's Kelly Tuck has placed a white rocking chair facing a painted, barred window. Matthew Hindly uses electronic surveillance equipment to time the moment that the viewer spends looking at his empty work. And that's it for images of security. Contrary to expectation, security contraptions are not the only objects that characterise the contradictions of the South African home.

Inspired by the writings of WEB du Bois, Durban's Thando Mama presents a self-portrait in video of himself watching television. Against a soundtrack of chatter about blackness nothing really happens, while the light from the video flickers on Mama's bare black skin. It is this sense of ennui that characterises much art of the moment. "It's an understated politics," MacKenny says. "It's a personal politics that relates to the country's politics, or its purported vision of itself. And it comes out of incredible constriction. In the Homing in show there's a lot of underlying debate or engagement with constriction and voicelessness, or attempts to find some kind of place to speak. In some cases the silences are the most articulate things there.

"I think there is a longing for home values. Home is a seriously contested arena, with the highest child abuse figures in the world, the highest crime rates in the world and the highest HIV in the world. All this is centred in the home. I think many of these works are quite negative reflections, but I don't think they're only negative. I think that the fact that it is being grappled with is positive."

This grappling doesn't always result in celebration. On its main stages the festival has presented work that portrays domestic life as riddled with conflict and betrayal. The South African home is a battleground and, as in group therapy, the cultural platform is providing an upsetting role play.

Jay Pather's *Home* takes its audience on a journey to nine locations where women are stressed breadwinners (Nelisiwe Rushualang dances with money literally pinned to her, to indicate her status as bread-winner), where a migrant labourer is forced to call a bed a home. Not surprising that memories emerge like cadavers from cupboards and from the wings. Regarding home life, there is much that South Africans would rather forget.

Families are falling apart in works by Pieter-Dirk Uys, Yael Farber and Chris Mann. Uys's play *Auditioning Angels* is a melodrama set against the crumbling infrastructure of the Johannesburg hospital, where Aids orphans have to be abducted by nurses in order for them to get the attention they deserve. Here, evidence of a troubling child rape turns out to be that of a sadomasochistic game played by pre-adolescents who've picked up tips from what they've seen on television.

There is an inherent irony in witnessing Uys, the tireless campaigner for freedom from any form of censorship, taking a moral stance on the type of sexual material available to South Africa's homes. But this is a new era, one in which leaders are calling for moral regeneration as part of the African renaissance dream. So it's not surprising that artists are questioning what values this regeneration should include while showing horrendous pictures of family life in decay. There's the tale of family murder in Farber's *Molora*, in which children set out to kill their mother to avenge their father's death. In turning the plot into a tale of forgiveness, Farber offers a plea to end what, in South Africa, has become a "cycle of blood for blood". While *Molora*'s bloody purging offers no solution, it hints at resolution. This is useful, given the storm in the teacup that raged around Chris Mann's *Thuthula*: Xhosa traditional leaders objected to Mann's portrayal of this Romeo-and-Juliet episode in Xhosa history, saying he should have consulted with them first. It has shown just how volatile the retelling of domestic history can be.

Finally two images by women stand out as cries for a sense of resolution around domestic issues. First there is *Snow White,* a video work by Standard Bank Young Artist Award winner Berni Searle. In it Searle, a large black woman, kneels naked, covered in flour while kneading dough. Like a robot she sways to and fro, devoid of personality — a victim of her task.

The second is a quilt produced by Helen Granville of the South African Quilters' Guild. It shows fragmented images of fire, and mass-produced images of wild animals stare out of its folds. It's called *The Rape of Zimbabwe's Farms*. It's part of a new cultural category: white protest craft. Consider this when next you decorate your home. **04.07**

Hail King Louis!

Tebogo Alexander

Louis Moholo is one of the world's greatest free drummers. Ample in personality, Moholo speaks forthrightly of the pain of exile and freedom, and his music — all of which are inextricably linked. The damp, grey London seeping into his small flat fails to dampen his passion for music. It's 1993, a week ahead of his first South African performance in nearly three decades, and the master drummer is excited as he anticipates performing before a home crowd.

Fast forward to a few weeks ago, literally a decade after that first meeting. Again, Moholo prepares for performance on home soil. This time we're in downtown Johannesburg, and the place is Nicki's Bar with its typical Friday-night buzz. The black professionals frequenting the watering hole fail to recognise the timekeeper often compared to Elvin Jones, a legend right up there with United States "stick masters" Roy Haynes and Max Roach.

Moholo is the last surviving member of the famed Blue Notes that featured saxophonist Dudu Pukwana, pianist Chris McGregor, bassist Johnny Dyani and trumpeter Mongezi Feza. This quintet arrived in Britain in the mid-Sixties with their own brand of jazz, which was influenced by traditional African folk music and the improvisational innovations of John Coltrane and Duke Ellington. It was a fusion that allowed them to fit into Europe's free jazz scene with ease.

London photographer Val Wilmer recorded their arrival and watched them invigorate the British jazz scene, which was lumbering under the strain of the big-band sounds in an era that changed to favour smaller bebop outfits. Wilmer observed that The Blue Notes "literally overturned the London jazz scene". It was the freedom to express that made the difference, observes Moholo. "Freedom made sense to me. I was looking for it all the time ... But it was in me before then but I didn't recognise it until I came to Europe."

On the surface, this 63-year-old pioneer is a simple lad from Langa with a passion for jazz. Not one to blow his own horn, but should the need arise he's quick to remind you of his stature. On another level, he's still the iconic father of London's South African jazz community, and since the death of his contemporaries he watches over the emerging talents of the next generation.

Watching the Friday evening go by over beer and memories, after the launch of the *Return to Roots* tour that will take place in Gauteng from June 13 to 16, Moholo tells of his pleasure at being home again. It may only be his second South African billing since leaving the country nearly 40 years ago, but it marks the closing of the circle that began when, under the shadow of the Sharpeville massacre in 1960, this country produced some of its most original music.

The circle begins to close with the emergence of a new generation of innovators in pianist Bheki Mseleku, saxophonist Zim Ngqawana, trumpeters Feya Faku and Marcus Wyatt, as well as pianist Andile Yenana. Add to them Moholo's London protégés in the Pheto brothers, Jibo (acoustic bass) and Pule Peto (piano), percussionists Thomas Dyani and Thebe Lepere and saxophonist Ntshukumo Bonga, who are mostly still abroad.

In recognition of the new generation's avant-garde flag-flying, Moholo has called on their talents for the *Return to Roots* tour.

Working with him will be the Pheto brothers, Faku, Wyatt, drummer Lulu Gontsana, saxophonists Khaya Mahlangu, Barney Rachabane, Robbie Jansen and acoustic bassist Herbie Tsoali. They share the platform with Londoners Steve Beresford (pianist), John Edwards (bassist), Francine Luce (vocalist) and Jason Yarde (saxophonist).

The seeds of Moholo's musical roots were planted by marching bands that often passed through Cape Town's townships. It was the guy in the front with the big bass drum that fascinated the aspiring drummer. "This cat used to excite me." It was while playing with legendary Cape saxophonist "Cups" Nkanuka's Cordettes in the mid-1950s that his destiny was decided.

Unfortunately, Moholo's entry into the professional ranks of music coincided with the tightening grip of Afrikaner nationalism. It was not long before Moholo and his drum set would be well-hidden behind curtains as he accompanied white musicians in Cape Town clubs. While this heavy atmosphere gave rise to two of the country's seminal bands, The Jazz Epistles and The Blue Notes, much of the talent would choose exile.

After all these years the rigours of exile manifest themselves on Moholo's aging features, none more so than when he speaks of Feza, who died from pneumonia in London in 1975. It was this prospect, it seems, that deterred more mature Blue Notes members of the original band. Bassist Dyani replaced a reluctant Sammy Maritz, while tenorman Nikele Moyake only made it to Switzerland before returning home when the rest of the band moved on to London. In some ways it was their youth that made it all an adventure. None were beyond their mid-twenties when Moholo, Pukwana, McGregor, Dyani and Feza arrived in London. These guys were more than just good friends. "There was no mother, no father, you're on your own black man."

In moving to the capital of Britain in the 1960s they were choosing to be situated in the world's mecca of music. "Everything was happening. The Beatles were here. Jimi Hendrix, The Rolling Stones, Wes Montgomery, you name them. Unlike in Switzerland where we upset the musicians because they were into the American stuff, we were into something else and they couldn't take us. But here, they could take us because were talking the same language."

Guitarist Wes Montgomery contributed to their breakthrough by recommending The Blue Notes to Ronnie Scott's, London's premier jazz venue. "We were lucky because there were a lot of people who came to Britain around the same time as we did who didn't make it."

Moholo was the first to break away from The Blue Notes, describing the parting as painful. Soon after the break-up he and Dyani joined saxophonist Steve Lacy and Enrico Rava for a gig in Argentina. For the South Africans, Argentina was the stepping stone to North America and eventually New York, where they hoped to link up with Albert Ayler. "When we went there, we were innovators. We were kings, I tell you. It was really nice to be in this position."

Returning to London The Blue Notes made the only recording featuring all five members. From there their paths separated. Moholo and Pukwana remained in London, McGregor finally settled in France, while Dyani chose Sweden, with Feza moving between the two countries. Looking back, Moholo regrets not spending more time on stage with Dyani. "I would have liked to have been with Johnny's band Witchdoctor's Son."

When Feza died, the remaining Blue Notes members held the wake in the studio, playing what Moholo was to describe as prayer music. "It was moving, very touching. You hear it in the music. It was really coming from the heart." The tradition continued when Dyani died in 1986. But 1991 saw the death of both Pukwana and McGregor, within weeks of each other, leaving Moholo empty outside of his music.

He is empty without his "blood brothers", but he knows the battle is far from over. The musical revolutionary that is King Louis is leading a new army, whose foot soldiers know that in the same way mental chains are breaking here at home, so must the musical barriers go down. **13.06**

"The use of our vehicles in the contexts is unacceptable to us and will result in a negative connotation being attached to our vehicles in the minds of viewers. This will in turn have a detrimental impact upon our brand and cause us to sustain damages." — Statement by BMW South Africa, on the use of its cars in the local movie, *Hijack Stories*, about gangsters in Jo'burg. 20.06

Pity he's Australian now

Editorial

So JM Coetzee missed out on a Booker Prize hat-trick this year but got the Nobel Prize for Literature. This is surprising, in that the Nobel committee has usually been seen to award the prize for quasi-ideological reasons — Aleksandr Solzhenitsyn, for instance, got it at a time when it was necessary to highlight oppression in the Soviet Union; Nadine Gordimer's award was an endorsement of democratic forces in South Africa.

That is not to say such winners are not great writers, but not since Samuel Beckett (one of Coetzee's key influences) got the prize in 1969 has it gone to an author so unattached to any cause, so pessimistic about the possibility of redemption, so sceptical about humanity's progress and its capacity for ethical action. In the mid-1980s in South Africa, as this country seemed locked in a terrible war between oppressors and liberators, Coetzee refused to allow his protagonist Michael K to join the freedom fighters. Unlike Nadine Gordimer's characters, who usually opted (though not without deep inner struggle) to join the forces of liberation, whatever their failures, Michael K decided instead to look after his vegetables. It is as though a novel such as *Life and Times of Michael K* operates in the gap of doubt present in Gordimer — the gap she closes but Coetzee leaves open, even widens. He took a lot of flak for that.

Likewise, Coetzee's most famous novel, *Disgrace*, and his first to be set explicitly in post-apartheid South Africa, is not a hopeful or comforting book. It seems to argue, via the shape of its narrative, that the promise of a new dispensation in South Africa — the promise of a new ethical space — is unfulfilled. It drew cries of baffled outrage from some of the less sophisticated readers in the African National Congress.

But Coetzee's relentless deconstruction of our self-delusions, including our pretensions to knowledge and mastery, rediscovers the fundamentals of our humanity in the quality of empathy. For that reason, and because he writes with such hard beauty, the award to him should be widely hailed in South Africa.

Pity he's an Australian now. We still need his limpid gaze. **03.10**

Art battles at the mall

François Ebersöhn

An African celebration by one of South Africa's most famous artists stands on the brink of destruction as hammers and drills await the word from developers bent on enlarging one of Johannesburg's richest shopping centres.

Cecil Skotnes put the finishing touches to his untitled mural at the entrance of Hyde Park Corner shopping centre 32 years ago. At the time he intended the work for its commissioned position: 100m in the air. But then the work was placed at ground level leaving its rough contours, planned with a certain distance in mind, to close scrutiny. That was not the end of the world, but Skotnes "lost interest" a couple of years later when the 40m-plus mural was "shortened" by more than a third to make way for doors to the shoppers' paradise.

Hyde Park Corner is one of the most expensive square kilometres of mixed residential and commercial real estate on the continent. It claims to be a "timeless recreation of modern elegance". Completed in 1969, it was the first fully enclosed decentralised shopping centre to be developed in South Africa.

For the next three decades the mural, situated next to an open air car park, would be shrouded in petrol fumes — its rough yet delicate figurines to be eventually blocked by luxury 4x4 vehicles of the super rich shopping crowd. All the while, through sunshine and rain, the characteristic ochre yellow and matte burgundy colours of Skotnes would fade away while inside the shopping centre the Edoardo Villa reclining bronze sculpture and the Guiseppe Cattaneo mural would do a disappearing act of another kind.

The Villa work very recently got a new owner — a private collector who apparently got fed-up with the constant moving around of the sculpture to make space for "other" exhibitions in the centre. Just last weekend this took the shape of motorcycles and a cigarette manufacturer of the cowboy variety who now markets itself as a clothing design label. The Cattaneo work has disappeared behind a wall in a restaurant somewhere under the Apollo Café and the Baldinelli mural has become a feast for the eyes only of cinema goers whose

136

bladders edge them to the toilets. And that's only the part not blocked by a life-size movie-poster. The Skotnes mural, even though it bears no title, is, like his wooden engravings, decidedly African — a reminder that, together with Villa and Cattaneo, Sydney Kumalo and Cecily Sash, he was part of a group of artists called "Amadlozi" or Spirit of the Forefathers. Together and separately these artists' works have been seen in countless exhibitions of note around the globe, among them biennales held from São Paulo to Florence.

Speaking from his home in Cape Town, the 77-year-old artist and acclaimed pioneer of modern art in South Africa was philosophical and took a "sober" view of the imminent demise of his only work not to be treated with tender love and care. Skotnes merely describes the work as decorative. Its original theme was that of a procession, alluded to by the shapes of people, but that was lost once the mural was broken up. "I'm not looking back with any anger," he mused, adding that he was having a bit of fun with the "status" conferred on the mural by having the discussion with the *Mail & Guardian* and others, such as his dealer Linda Givon (owner of the Linda Goodman Gallery).

Until last week Givon and the developers of the shopping centre were contemplating ways to save the mural. Bram Joynt, the architect involved in the development, was adamant that a way would be found to preserve the work, although some scepticism seeped through during the discussion. Removing the sculptured plaster would be out of the question since its thickness never stretches beyond a mere centimetre or two while, at close inspection, the brick work underneath actually makes its appearance in places. That leaves a cast as a possibility, but neither the artist nor his dealer is happy with that. In fact, last weekend Givon changed her mind completely, sharing Skotnes's unwillingness to have anything to do with saving the work and adding that the battered old wall and destruction by pollution has turned it into an insult to the artist.

Perhaps something could still be done. It is a significant piece of work, even if it was "pruned", said celebrated art historian Esmé Berman, who has just returned from the United States where she has lived for the past 16 years. She recalls how a forgotten Diego Rivera mural on a patio of a private home in Los Angeles was recently discovered. The whole wall plus encasement was moved.

Skotnes was the most prominent of his artistic generation, his work had an African quality and his working method of *sgrafitto* dates back to the renaissance, Berman noted. Derived from the Italian word *sgraffiare* or "scratched away", *sgrafitto* adds a pattern by carving through or scraping off the uppermost layer of plaster to reveal inlayed portions of coloured cement. (Very finely graded cement was also applied during the day, which was then painted on while it was wet. The plastered section would then be cut with a knife to reveal the figures.) Skotnes is equally adept in the political arena where he played a leading role in opposing apartheid.

Perhaps the artist should have the last word in what could be dubbed the politics of the mall: Skotnes said he would be willing to do a new mural. **22.08**

In awe of balls and batterers

Zebulon Dread

On Monday night, while watching the descent of doom on Kingsmead and witnessing the collective South African psyche sink into the quagmire of the deep, dark abyss, I could not help but recall the words of Bob Marley, who sang: "Emancipate yourself from mental slavery for none but ourselves can free our mind ... don't be afraid of atomic energy, because none of them can stop Jah [God's] time."

While the cameras trawled and panned the ocean of depression as manifested in the noticeably dejected body language, I saw, in the drenching, salivating and drooling rain the marked face of an utterly amused Fate/Providence/Reality, who relished pissing on the grand parade of mediocrity, madness and false hope embodied by the International Cricket Council month of mental mayhem.

It was far from the emancipation spoken of by Marley. It was also the months of Lotto mayhem with queues snaking around the country as we submerged our minds, pockets and hopes in the possibility of becoming an instantly gratified son of capitalism with lots of capital to, forever, change our lives.

This time the Lotto was called cricket and we were all hoping, again, to be salvaged by our gladiators. I could not help but reminisce about the gladiatorial arena while watching our ovals fill to the brim with the savagely false hope that would/should/could cut us loose from the feeling of despair, despondency, hankering and lamenting for all that we want while doing little to achieve our desires. Instant gratification. The McDonald's of our dreams, the Wimpys of our desires and the Kentuckys of our hopes. Fast foods, fast solutions and a fast life to nowhere.

African renaissance? Upliftment of the people through the power of balls flung, hit, thrashed, thrown or kicked? Twenty-seven years of incarceration and our New Messiah, Madiba and his thousand-and-one cohorts, feeding the people the false hope of salvation while the Middle East and her messiahs have kept us hoping since time immemorial with no arrival time for the saviour.

The Lion called Fate intervened in our collective madness and devoured our gladiators, role models and mediocre flingers and batterers of balls into submission as they sat stunned by the awesome reality of their loss. How I wished we could feel that depressed and awed by the reality of Aids. I hoped, quietly, that our business community and economic saviours could plunge so much money into poverty relief. I wished that we could become that stunned by the interminable abuse of our children, women and old people. I wondered if we could ever feel that devastated by the continuing existence of racism in our midst.

I wrapped myself in the hope that we could feel that exhausted by the absolute environmental vilification by our brothers and sisters. I wanted to think we had enough regard for each other's humanity to weep together at the cataclysms of war, famine and drought that assail our brothers and sisters universally. It was not to be. Following the success of the "holy cow protectors", India, against the "unholy cow eaters", Pakistan, cities from Allahabad to Delhi and Bombay were embroiled in the goading of Muslims by dint of the prowess of one Tendulkar against one Waqar. A few cars were burnt, some people were stabbed and many cowered in their homes, hoping the madness would end.

The power of the little ball even had the whole of India stumped for a public holiday with schools closed for this epic battle against the arch-enemy. The scenes of jubilation were indicative of the resentment residing in the deeper recesses of India for their neighbour. Do I see Ali Bacher smile and spin his way out of it by dint of the incredible exposure, success and prominence the tournament has brought for all of our benefit? Do we hear the grandiose arguments again and again for the value of tourism? Are we again to hear the bullshit delivered from the political domain, with its minimal successes, as to the absolute importance of this orgy of balls so that the nation can feel proud? Blah, blah, fucken blah!

As for India and her little ball throwers and batterers, the tournament is already won by that significant defeat and all other failures are momentarily forgotten in the groundswell of patriotic pride that has given politicians new fervour to their speeches as the crumpled lives mired in the darkness of poverty from Calcutta to Bombay are forgotten in this great conquest. Who said sport is not political?

I return to Ncgonde Balfour's question: "Who is Jacques Kallis?" and ask, indeed, who are our cricketers? Who are these gladiators whom we have sacrificed in the international arena to salvage our national pride? Who are these young pups whom we have thrown in front of the hurricane from down under who continually drench us in shame, scorn and derision? Who, indeed, is Shaun Pollock? What is his value to this renaissance, this good Christian with his goodly Christian values? How will he and the rest save us from ourselves? Is his ball battering and bowling to be our new Messiah? Or is it young Paul Adams, Mr Zondeki or even Mr Ntini?

Has everyone forgotten this is simply a bloody fucken stupid little sport played by mundane, middle-class, often mediocre, individuals whose only worth is that they are good batterers or bowlers of a little ball flung between six sticks from one end of the field to another? Have we forgotten this "sport", of very little real value, would be nothing of prominence if not for the excessive spending of advertising-hungry corporates who sit and wait for opportunities to increasingly colonise our consumerist tendencies and who gratifyingly add to this nonsensical hype with their only real *raison d'être* being the possibility of our becoming their usable slaves?

Think, for a moment, of what, apart from all the S'effricans, cricket, kangaroos and abused Aborigines, you consider worthy of remembering about Australia? Feeling vacuous? The blandness of Australia is epidemic and, without sport, specifically cricket, they've got little to cheer about, mate, hence their exuberant enjoyment of conquering everyone with little balls and their infantile behaviour when doing so.

This is what we must emulate? This boisterous, boyish world of wanking sport! Nemesis or Messiah? It's been in our homes, our minds and our consciousness for quite some time and we've experienced a barrage of assault from the media who, in the absence of the intelligence needed to tackle many of the real issues at hand, have gorged themselves on tiresome speculations with regard to all that is and will be the cricket World Cup.

We've been fed such a diet of opinions ranging from trite to banal, repetitive and sometimes incredibly inane, that a wholesome relieving diarrhoea could not make us feel better had we managed to defecate from our bowels the whole caboodle, and yet none has been able to answer a simple question, which is whether our players are good enough to wrest this munificent, magnificent and stultifyingly obscene trophy from the Great Kangaroos who came here with their yellow train, kangaroo jumps — watch Brett Lee after taking a wicket — and amusing confidence, which, if truth be told, is much more than any of our local wimps could muster.

The answer is no! No, you cretinous mass of self-deluded hysteria desperate for some mental time-out to make yourselves feel better. No. They were never good enough. If you wish to play these inane games in the inane international arena where it is mostly advertising revenue that gives any of them any semblance of self-worth, you have to be brutal, self-confident and irritatingly egotistical so that you do not choke when it counts. It is not the arena of prayers to messianic saviours, but the domain of devils who love nothing more than winning for the sheer sake of winning. Just ask Australia if they pray before a game!

Throughout this miserable wretch of legal international money laundering we could see their bowling, batting, mental fitness and just plain ability was lacking and that the mass hysteria created by the media is largely to blame for this "catastrophe". They were placed on pedestals they didn't earn or deserve and expectations were demanded of them that they were not ready for.

It is time to become a nation of honesty and show pride in our developmental achievements by nurturing the vast scope of talents possessed by our beloved country so that we emancipate our arts, sport, economy — big and small — to levels where one form of entertainment is not blown out of proportion so as to present us with the cascading waterfall of false hope that we see evident in so many layers of our society.

Remember the soccer World Cup? The rugby World Cup? The mass of expectations? Speaking to an acquaintance, Doctor Peter Ashman, a community health psychiatrist, we mused on this state of limbo and the concomitant level of expectation created out of the decrepit idea that something must save us.

He, learned doctor that he is, was amazed and questioned himself regularly as to why he was wasting time watching this useless crap knowing it was a ripe recipe for depression. Another set-up within the domicile of false hopes. We shared the feeling of amusement at the excruciating level of despair that filled the stadium in those last moments. Laughed at the many ifs and buts flung around by commentators paid to flirt with speculation while the heavens were merciless with their wet vomit.

I have learnt one valuable lesson from this monstrosity and that is that we are still a nation of liars, pretenders to the throne and easily deluded by those with agendas not worthy of human exploration. I have seen that we think nothing of wasting millions of rands in the pursuit of our vainglorious ideals while procrastinating on the simple issues of providing our sick and dying with basic care.

I have seen that we still have our heads so far up the anus of the United States and Europe that we think these arenas, where our gladiators do battle in the games of the "colonisers", will give us the power to lift our finger in a collective up-yours, stimulate our consciousness or give us the strength to carry on.

I have seen that our high-flying president, Citizen Number One, proliferates this madness in his personal pursuit to find acceptance for his intellect, ideas and diplomacy while being unable to find even a simple solution or conclusion to a simple disease, while all we, the people and owners of him and his gorgeous aircraft, want him to do is deal with the absolute responsibility of truly rebuilding this wasteland left to us by the legacy of madness that was apartheid, thus helping us to find the wings which are waiting in the deeper recesses of the heart where true love dwells, waiting to be mined for our eternal evolution. Love of each as we should love ourselves. True healing not through slogans and hype, but through endeavour and real assistance that will bring everyone into the framework of humanity without shame.

Sport is really a minute and pissy inconsequential part of this evolution. The reality of the African renaissance is that we must all start engaging in the "sport" of friendship, trust, love, compassion, nurturing and true African *ubuntu*. I am amused and wonder who is batting the ball that is Thabo being flung hither and thither.

Hau! Ma Afrika! Aluta Continua! **07.03**

LETTERS
Relax, Mr Dread

Zebulon Dread should consider the definition of a "false dichotomy": the fallacious assertion that one (desirable) choice of action precludes another. An example of this is asserting that one cannot be both depressed about South Africa's exit from the cricket World Cup and concerned about other pressing social problems. Most cricket fans are both. I am sure even the self-righteous Mr Dread spends some of his time doing things for relaxation that are as arbitrary as the "battering of and bowling of balls" and are not wholly aimed at uplifting the poor, saving Aids babies or ending crime. — *Nick Ferreira, Melville, 14.02*

Peace is more important than play

Zebulon Dread's article was spot on. Whatever happened to magnanimity in victory, and graciousness in defeat? Or the Olympic ideal of simply participating? Our priorities are way off, and it's only when we knuckle down and concentrate on what's really important that we'll become a winning nation. Would we rather be remembered for winning a sports match or for becoming a shining example of peace, prosperity and justice? — *WL Mason, Johannesburg*

Zebulon, you foolish man. You overlook the fact that millions of people simply love cricket. Such is the game's beauty that politicians, corporate egos, global capital, media thugs, crooked players and infantile administrators have not yet wholly managed to obscure it. Thankfully, nor have you. — *Mark Mattson, Durban*

What was the point of the recent contributions by Zebulon Dread? Or rather: what is the point of Zebulon Dread? — *Jacques Rousseau, Cape Town, 20.03*

Fighting for the Lord

Gavin Foster

His ring record was impressive. At 16 he was the youngest amateur heavyweight boxing champion in the country. Of the 28 professional heavyweight fights under his substantial belt when he retired at the age of 27 Jimmy Abbott had won 25 on knockouts and lost three on points, without ever being knocked down. He'd put an end to Kallie Knoetze's career by knocking the South African heavyweight champion, ranked fifth in the world, right out of the ring to deprive him of his title in the first round. But the public loved to hate him, with every appearance in the ring being greeted by jeers and catcalls.

Abbott was larger than even a heavyweight boxer should be, and the press christened him the "Dancing Doughnut" and the "Bouncing Blimp". His out-of-the-ring shenanigans also attracted attention, as did the ministrations of his father, an interfering ex-boxer who was not known for his diplomacy.

When Abbott fought Eddie "The Animal" Lopez in Durban the journalists started sharpening their pencils. First there was an uproar when Abbott senior unexpectedly brought Jimmy's wife down to Durban, where she discovered that her husband was ensconced in a local hotel suite with a girlfriend. The ugly scene that followed made front-page headlines.

Then, in the ring, a battered Abbott returned to his corner between rounds to be reduced to tears when his father launched a secondary barrage of blows upon his head for not fighting properly. I ask him about the incident and he laughs. "Hey, you remember that? He gave me a lekker couple of smacks in my corner. He was fighting outside with other people while I was fighting in the ring. That was one of the fights I lost on points." Boxing was interesting in those days.

But things are different for 42-year-old Abbott now. The man who started out as a railway ticket examiner and went on to be a world-ranked boxer despite his unprepossessing physique is now a pastor and faith healer with the Apostolic Faith Mission. He's reduced his weight from 310kg to 140kg, and spends his time spreading the word of God.

Abbott says that his fate was preordained. "My mother made a promise on the day that I was born that she would give the child inside her to the Lord. My father had hit her, and she was lying there in her blood begging God to let her child live. She gave me to the Lord when I was born. Later on my wife started praying that I would come to the Lord, and God changed my life."

So what triggered the transition from sinner to saint? "After I gave up boxing I became a professional wrestler, known as The Viking. One day I was sitting thinking about it, and I realised it was all false. Wrestling is the biggest lie on earth. It's a joke — rubbish. We'd sit in the dressing room and plot who was going to win, then we'd go out and wrestle and the crowds would go crazy. I couldn't live with myself like that and that's when the Lord started speaking to me."

So, cheating on your wife was okay, but cheating the public wasn't? "Well, I wasn't cheating very much on my wife. But, you see, when you're wrestling you always have fans running after you, mainly women." Sadly, Abbott's 24-year marriage to Carrie now seems over. The wife who forgave his love for other women couldn't handle his obsessive love for God and left earlier this year. "She couldn't take all the church and the miracles and things. She prayed for me to change and work for the Lord, but now I'm doing that, with all the miracles and wonders, she's not happy. She's my heart's desire after the Lord, and I'd love to have her back, but if she interferes with my work I'll carry on on my own."

Miracles and wonders? When I first met Abbott a couple of years ago he told me that he was "curing the sick, healing the lame and raising the dead". The question begs to be asked. "That's it!" he enthuses. "I've prayed for four people who were certified dead, laid my hands on them and prayed, and God restored their lives!" It turns out that none of the four was, strictly speaking, actually dead at the time of the healing, but all had apparently been written off by doctors and recovered after Abbott's prayers. Abbott also travels to prisons around the country preaching to inmates and was the first person to baptise prisoners.

This sparks a memory, and I ask about his brother whom I remember reading was convicted of murder recently. "Oh, my two brothers," he says. "Ricky and Charlie are both in for murder — Charlie's served about six or seven years already and Ricky was convicted this year. But I can tell you, they've changed. They've met the Lord Jesus Christ."

Abbott's not really interested in boxing anymore — he thinks that it's become too much like wrestling, with hype and money dominating the numerous championships — but he can be fiercely protective of his religious convictions. Three years ago he challenged the speaker of the Eastern Cape legislature to a round in the ring after he said that Jesus Christ was a communist. "He never came back to me," says Abbott. "I would have made an example of him using the Word of God. But if he'd put the gloves on I'd have clobbered him to hospital." Would that have been wise? "I suppose not — people would have said that Jimmy Abbott hadn't changed one bit. I also took on that singer, Steve Hofmeyr. He called my Jesus Christ a loser and said that if Bart Simpson was God he'd have created a better world than God did." Hofmeyr wisely didn't respond.

One man who could get Abbott back into the ring for a full go is Mike Tyson. "I'd love that," he says. "I'd train for a good fight and every time I hit him I'd preach the Word of God to him."

So does the man the public loved to hate feel more loved nowadays? "Oh yes. What I'm doing now is a hundred, a thousand times, better than anything I ever did before. Some still hate me, but they all remember me." **11.04**

Mills & Boon meets the gynae

Julia Beffon

Several years ago, when I was first starting out as a daily newspaper journalist, my news editor sent me out on one of the silliest stories to which I've ever been assigned. His briefing was a bit vague: a couple who had been trying unsuccessfully to have a child for several years had discovered nudism and, as a result, were now expecting a baby.

The address was for a large house in the northern suburbs of Johannesburg, so I was unsurprised by the electric gates and the large dogs. I was, however, completely thrown when the front door was opened by a totally naked middle-aged man and his equally naked and extremely pregnant wife.

The photographer and I were ushered into the lounge, where we were offered tea and biscuits and treated as though interviewing naked people was a regular occurrence on a mid-week afternoon.

I was gripped by that exquisite embarrassment felt only by the fully clothed in the presence of the totally naked. By selecting a very low chair and using the biscuits to bribe their Pyrenean mountain dog to stand in front of me so that all I could see was the couple's heads above its huge back, I was able to get through the interview with a degree of sanity.

What this couple wanted to share with my newspaper — and through it the world — was that by converting to nudism the husband had rid himself of his tight-fitting underpants, thereby raised his sperm count and this had resulted in the wife finally falling pregnant. I heard about all this in much greater detail than I required.

On leaving their opulent home I felt a degree of irritation, bordering on resentment, that I'd been subjected to their story — and thought sourly that, had the husband merely chosen to wear looser-fitting underpants, I'd have been spared.

Nearly 20 years later, while watching a new South African-made sex education video, I got a similar attack of the galloping mother-grundies. The video in question is *Expanded Orgasm for Her,* the first in a planned series from Endless Pleasure. Self-styled sensualist Jonti Searll and video-production duo Kevin and Tanya Factor are behind this venture, which, they believe, will teach adults some techniques to improve their love lives.

The "Pleasure Box" package includes the video, the CD *Music for Making More than Love*, a water-based lubricant and a candle. (I, too, first thought that these last two items might be used in conjunction with each other — but rest assured, the candle is merely to provide lighting when creating a romantic ambience.) The idea is fabulous. From my limited personal experience of South African men's lovemaking techniques, anything that would teach them some new tricks is welcome.

The problem — as is so often the case in matters of a sexual nature — is in the execution. The promotional material promises that the video will teach you how to give a woman an orgasm that lasts for up to 30 minutes. The point of the expanded orgasm is to prolong the sensual experience by delaying — or, in the case of the video, avoiding — climax. But the "lesson" is so dry and joyless that I can't imagine anyone wanting to rush to bed to try out what they've learned. Put it this way, you're more likely to want a cup of cocoa than a cold shower.

For *Expanded Orgasm for Her* is not at all erotic. It shows in clinical detail the correct techniques for manual stimulation of the clitoris and vagina, complete with a serious voice-over, "mood" music and, incongruously, several sequences of waves rolling up a beach. In all, the impression is of Mills & Boon meets gynaecological exam. To end off with, you're treated to a Searll seminar, with devotees sitting around cross-legged on a carpet listening to the guru expound on how his techniques have helped save many marriages.

This quasi-mysticism and the evangelical zeal on the part of the publicists are what brought the Jo'burg nudists to mind. And this time, there wasn't a Pyrenean mountain dog to shelter behind. **14.02**

> "Even if the struggle was about sex, as the management portrays it, students are, without apologising, entitled to have sex." — "Malcolm X" of the Pan-African Student Movement of Azania, commenting on protests at Technikon Witwatersrand over new restrictions on overnight guests at residences. 22.08

A little wet dream problem

Bismarck Masangu

Resolutions are a joke, wet dreams are not. For now cleaning up my closet has taken precedence over getting rid of the bulge. You see, last night I had an erotic dream that painted me in a compromising position with another man. Although I woke up just before I was assaulted by the graphic pictures of anal penetration, I did find my middle stump unabashedly excited.

I was shell-shocked, appalled and confused, but mainly bowled over that my heterosexual integrity is, nay, was, not a completely resolved matter. In fact, my initial reaction was to bolt in the opposite direction and shag the first accommodating trollop.

Then I thought, perhaps I should bombard myself with a deluge of gay porn just to check if it would have the same lecherous effect while I was conscious. As you can gather, I felt like someone holding a key for which there is no door. My confusion was akin to that of a cricketer who dreams of batting for the other side, or a chaste woman — whatever that is — who is appalled to have a wet dream in which she is consensually deflowered by a group of priapic male studs.

And to confound matters further, such dreams — especially those that involve involuntary nocturnal emissions — exact an unhealthy psychological hold on the dreamer that makes it embarassing or imprudent to talk about them to anyone who is not a psychiatrist.

Speaking of shrinks, haven't they already conned us into believing the gospel according to Saint Freud which states that (profane) dreams are nothing but the portentous Trojan horse of repressed wishes and desires? Hence, any attempt at dream analysis is deemed a dereliction of duty if, as the penetrating essayist Gore Vidal aptly noted, "no Freudian cliché is left unstroked".

According to this school of thought, a woman who dreams of herself being raped longs on a subconcious level to be violated. In fact, such is the sneering assumptions of the Freudians that they will allege that my compromising wet dream is not a mere a freak of the mind, but the unimpeachable symptom of my "latent homoerotic inclination". Which is to say, in plain English, that I am a closet moffie!

Any attempt at denial will be met by the smug retort that nothing happens in a vacuum. Thus, I will be compelled to come to terms with what professional opinion terms my "homosexual feminist compulsion" — I cried when Mufasa died in *The Lion King*; have a kinky predilection for being squashed into that posture of defeat during the missionary position; and I am guilty of curiously wondering how it would feel to sleep with another man. Also, this compulsion will be used to explain why, despite my caveman pedigree, I was quite understanding — and not forceful — when, in the heat of passion, my partner suddenly decided to substitute sex for a cuddle.

By extension this compulsion may, perhaps, explain in a roundabout way why I court women who fall into the untapped market category because they do not register a blip on the *Cosmopolitan* radar — due to either corpulence, ugliness or melanin-charged complexions. Apparently, rather than deal with my "latent homoerotic inclination" I am compelled to prey on women with "issues" as they are not spoilt for choice and tend to accept any proposal that comes their way.

Technically speaking, the cavalier sentiment of the smug Freudians does not hold water. For, just as a person is not deemed to be either suicidal or a hunger striker after missing one meal, one does not automatically qualify as an alcoholic after gulping one beer. *A priori*, one queer dream does not promote or degrade — take your pick — me to homosexuality.

Allow me to digress. Consciously, I would say that I am about as attracted to other men as a magnet to wood. To wit, I refuse to be drawn into the jejune arguments of whether Denzel Washington is sexy or handsome, or to pass judgement on the kneaded posterior mound of Brad Pitt.

Anyway, was the dream a revelation, a fantastical manifestation, or the kind of confession you get in a nightmare of what you have done in the past? I imagine my mind was just mimicking the smut orgies of pornographic flicks, but I do not know for certain.

What I do know for certain is that dreams — like drought, cancer and Robert Mugabe — are not sentimental. Indeed, trying to find rhyme and reason in these phenomena is tantamount to trying to find a corner inside a rondavel. In that vein, I have resolved to take this dream like a man by dismissing it as a disagreeable blur before

I court psychosis and end up like those poor sods who continually receive "winning" Lotto numbers from "the gods" in their dreams.

And correct me if I am wrong, but isn't sleeping about making your way to actualities by waking up to the arbitrariness of things?
14.03

Gay dreams bruise straight egos

Xolisa Vitsha

Homoeroticism is despised by most heterosexual men because it seems to challenge their own heterosexuality — and Bismarck Masangu's "A little wet dream problem" is typical. His article testifies to the truism that the only area in society where sameness is reviled is in the area of sexuality. He feels the need to probe whether the dream defines his sexual identity. The homosexual dream is not enough to determine his sexual identity. It is, however, intriguing that Masangu is shocked and disgusted over the dream and exhausts himself (and his readers) in explaining why the dream says nothing, nothing, about his proclivities.

Like Masangu I consider myself a straight guy. On reading Masangu's dilemma, I began thinking about what my response would have been to a homosexual dream. I was horrified to realise I would have probably reacted the same way, ending up in a dialogue with myself to be convinced of my heterosexuality as well. But surely, I've berated myself, one cannot have one dream and wake up with a different sexual identity? What then does Masangu's wet dream represent?

In today's terms, sexual orientation is defined separately from sexual identity. Laura Reiter, a psychologist, defines a homosexual as an adult whose fantasies, attachments and longings are predominantly for persons of the same gender, who may or may not express those longings in overt behaviour, and whose orientation may or may not be accompanied by a homosexual identity. This definition may be extended to heterosexuals and bisexuals.

Recent research acknowledges that both homosexual and heterosexual activities may occur coincidentally in a single period in the life of a single individual. If Masangu had also had this understanding of sexual orientation, he would not have made a fuss about whether the dream qualified him for or disqualified him from homosexuality.

This understanding of sexual orientation means that at one point in time one may have a proclivity towards the same gender without transforming self-understanding as heterosexual. It is therefore irrelevant for me to be thinking of the dream as defining, even in the slightest sense, my sexual identity. Sexual orientation may also not be cast in stone. It may be a shifting state of being while one may consciously keep one identity.

The issue that I or Masangu should be contending with is the feeling of discomfort that the dream brings. This discomfort emanates more from homophobic cultural socialisation. This is the very thing that makes homoerotic fantasies shameful to heterosexual males while there is an expression of desire that erupts in the realm of dreams.

Masangu would like to view the dream as a "mere freak of the mind", an isolated incident. This is because we would rather be dreaming of ourselves "conquering" women. To find ourselves protagonists in homosexual fantasies is a bruise on our culturally acquired masculine ego. Dreams are complex and sophisticated psychological processes that cannot be dismissed. The wet dream may represent the homoerotic "wonder" of many heterosexual men, of what it might be like to be homosexual.

The argument that sexual orientation may shift and that young adolescents tend to respond to both heterosexual and homosexual stimuli agrees with my opinion that if my first sexual experience is heterosexual or homosexual, then my feelings will be oriented in that particular preference. This may shift in heterosexuals leading to a "socialisation of desire" that means that the direction of desire may change. Masangu's discussion of his wet dream does not understand these dynamics of human sexuality. It is a shock response to the homoerotic fantasy and a way of dealing with the discomfort it brought. My advice to my brother: don't be scared! **02.05**

My big fat Afrikaner wedding

Yolandi Groenewald

Afrikaner weddings provide an equal chance of becoming the party of the year or the most grotesque event the guests have ever attended. And the main actors often feel the same way: the wedding is either the best day in the married couple's lives, or they burn all the pictures and pretend it never happened.

Afrikaner culture has a minefield of customs and traditions that may leave the bride and groom wondering why they didn't head to Mauritius for an anonymous beach ceremony. That choice will itself break a slew of tribal taboos, a calumny that will bring down the wrath of their extended family at every braai they attend for the rest of their lives.

Planning the wedding starts the day you are born. Your grandmother, who may not survive to your wedding day, will happily deposit her finest Africana teacups into your dowry kist to get the process started. The delicately painted scenes of Bloedrivier and the Transvalia Vierkleur on the cups are only suitable for proper children of the volk.

Church is an important factor in the life of a good Afrikaner family. Like the Voortrekker Monument, it is a hulking part of your past, something you try to escape in the present, but know you won't be able to shed in the future.

Though the three sister churches — the Gereformeerde Kerk, better known as the Doppers, the Dutch Reformed Church (NG Kerk) and the Hervormde Kerk — basically preach the same Calvinist values, they must not be confused with each other.

My father is a *stoere* (unflinching) Dopper and was all for keeping this faith down the family line to eternity. This argument disappeared like wine at a Dopper communion when my hubby-to-be revealed that his father was a dominee in the NG Kerk — a dominee's kids count at least double in the marital stakes, whatever the minor ecclesiastical peccadilloes laid on their parents.

The church business gets even more complicated if the vestal virgin and her eligible boereseun decide to move in together before exchanging their marital vows. Tannies wink at each when they pass the fallen couple at the weekly service. Sunday after Sunday the dominee will urge the congregation to pray for those living in sin as the perps cringe in embarrassment.

Announce your engagement and a finely tuned machine incorporating mothers, tannies, cousins and oumas springs into action. Ouma soon lets you know that no chic, satanic, one-stop venue may even be contemplated instead of the Old Dopper kerk where she was married.

Those who have been living in sin soon realise they cannot hope to get away with a white wedding. The tannies' gimlet eyes would strip the white dress off your frame as you waltzed down the aisle. But if your sins were less obvious, wearing anything other than white would set tongues wagging. I pleased my mother and went with the virgin white ensemble she had dreamed about before I was even a twinkle in anyone's eye.

Don't consider anything but the most extravagant wedding: every single relative, no matter how removed, is an honoured guest. This is your parents' last opportunity to brag and nothing but the best will do, though the expense could have set you up for life in a riverfront mansion rather than the one-room flatlet you land in.

Obscure members of the extended family should be expected to turn your wedding into a fiasco. Tannie Katryn may not be seated at the same table as her ex-husband Oom Os, because he has found himself a new heifer that Tannie Katryn is none too fond of. Oom Kees has promised to eviscerate his estranged wife's new lover, and she insists on bringing him along. The rest of the family waits with glee to witness the confrontation; you can only pray that the postal service will lose at least one of their invitations.

An Afrikaner wedding is based on the sound theology of a good party, which demands copious quantities of suitable liquor. My husband paid a king's ransom to ensure that no guests would be left dry. We restricted the hooch to wine and beer because we had seen the fallout after Klippies was introduced to wedding parties. One couple we met at varsity took the plunge before us. The police had to break up a fight between the groom and bride's well-lubricated families after they fought over her chastity.

The success of any Afrikaner wedding is measured against the culinary delights dished up at the reception. Afrikaners are carnivores and a lamb spit guarantees instant fame. I didn't even consider vegetarian cuisine, seen as an expression of confusion and self-hatred. A vegetarian friend and her husband decided to enforce their culinary preference on their guests — the wedding is still trotted out as an example of *volksverraad* (treason to the *volk*).

Good food and good dop cannot fail to impress Afrikaner guests, who will excuse wilted flowers and the skedonk you call a wedding car. A stuffed guest will forgive anything, even a dominee who keeps them inside the zinc-roofed church for more than two hours in the sweltering heat of a December afternoon. **17.04**

LETTERS
Big fat Afrikaner wedding memories

"My big fat Afrikaner wedding"— so Afrikaans! We all have Tannie Katryn, Oom Kees and other characters our family would like to hide in Timbuktu. Alas, we do need to see them once in a lifetime, even if it happens to be our wedding. I can't wait to read Yolandi Groenewald's next article! But for now my Calvinist values force me to return to my desk and start working. — *Mareli van der Walt, assistant editor, CellMag*

It was so true. Looking back, I did not enjoy my wedding day at all. Today I would do it in Spain or anywhere else, but for sure not the *stoere boere* thing. I enjoyed Groenewald's article very much. — *Manda Cronje*

Yolandi, ag nee. Jou artikel is soos 'n mes in my hart. Êrens het jy baie seergekry en ek kan nie glo dat jy jouself so met 'n sweep slaan nie. Ek het al baie troues bygewoon in die Afrikaner-milieu, en nêrens het ek so iets teegekom nie. Ek is trots op my kultuur en ek glo dat soos jou lewensondervinding groei, sal jy nie met baie trots terugkyk na hierdie artikel nie. — *Hendrik van Niekerk, 02.05*

Sea Point 'unrecognisable' as gangs move in

Marianne Merten

Police and members of Cape Town's gay community now believe the gory massacre at the Sizzlers massage parlour in Sea Point last week was a message from Cape Town gangs who felt their turf was being invaded. The massacre occurred shortly after Cape Town announced a bumper tourist festive season. But the murders have revealed another side of the Mother City — an underworld of gangs and drugs that has steadily crept from the Cape Flats to other areas in the peninsula as prostitution, protection rackets and narcotics provide lucrative markets throughout the city. A memorial service was held last Saturday at the local Anglican church for the "Graham Road Nine", as those murdered at Sizzlers have become known.

Only one victim survived the massacre. Seven people were found dead in the little white house at 7 Graham Road after the survivor stumbled to a local garage and raised the alarm. Two others died later in hospital. Most of the young victims came from across South Africa to escape poverty and were aged between 17 and 24; only the owner and a client were in their fifties.

There appeared to be little doubt among the mourners that the murders were connected with organised crime. The brutality — all the victims were tied up and most had their throats slit before being shot at point-blank range — was meant to set an example, they said. These types of execution-style killings are unfamiliar in the white areas of Cape Town, but regularly occur in the gang-dominated Cape Flats. Police are now investigating the involvement of gangs operating in the drug underworld, including gangs from Johannesburg. This week it emerged that Cape detectives have been in touch with their counterparts in Gauteng and are also tapping into police intelligence networks.

Sea Point occupies a special place in the city: its Jewish and gay communities are well established, and it has been a haven for black South Africans since the apartheid years. A strong middle-class presence remains because property prices are high thanks to Sea Point's proximity to both beach and city. This means those with money mingle with street prostitutes, who tout for dollar-rich tourists. Some of the priciest hotels in Cape Town stand near budget dives and properties from which slum landlords make a quick buck.

But Sea Point's connection with the drug underworld is not a new phenomenon. It was already an open secret in 1996 that Hard Livings gang boss Rashied Staggie had moved to the suburb from his home turf of Manenberg on the Cape Flats. His house at 3 Conifer Road, around the corner from Sizzlers, was a drug outlet. Police raided it several times, confiscating Mandrax, crack and dagga. The house was severely damaged in a pipe bomb attack in the early hours of New Year's Day 1997. But it was only in October 1998 that local police served notices threatening to confiscate it. Their attention caused the gang to shut up shop in Conifer Road and at the nearby Kingway hotel, which the Hard Livings had turned into a brothel.

Meanwhile, in moved other Cape Flats gangs, such as the Americans and the powerful drug cartel The Firm, which controls the countrywide Mandrax distribution networks. Nigerian groups, which control much of the cocaine and crack market in Gauteng, also established a base in the suburb, albeit subordinate to the powerful Cape Flats gangs.

By 1999 it was clear that private security company boss Cyril Beeka, said to be linked to alleged Mafia mobster Vito Palazzolo through interests in the central Cape Town clubland, had extended his reach into Sea Point. There he had allegedly teamed up with Staggie and The Firm to bolster their position in the face of violent clashes with People against Gangsterism and Drugs.

In November 1999 a pipe bomb rocked the gay Blah Bar, injuring nine; in August 2000 a car bomb exploded outside Bronx, a gay club; and in June 2000 two people were injured in an explosion at New York Bagels. None of these cases has been solved.

In the wake of last week's murders, questions are being asked about the lack of a local police presence, particularly because resources concentrated in the nearby Waterfont and central Cape Town have displaced crime into surrounding areas such as Sea Point. "Sea Point is unrecognisable from what it was five years ago," said one long-time resident.

Most residents had noted the increase in crime and lack of official willingness to deal with it beyond removing visible signs like street people. Last year's deployment of the municipal police became a joke as they merely handed out traffic citations. **31.01**

The two men arrested in connection with the Sizzlers massacre will go on trial in the Cape High Court in February 2004. Taxi driver Trevor Basil and waiter Adam Woest face nine counts of murder, one of attempted murder, counts of illegally possessing a weapon and ammunition and a charge of aggravated robbery and theft of vehicle. The two were declared fit to stand trial after a period of psychiatric observation in June. Shortly after their arrest in February they confessed to the extrodinarily brutal killings.

SA's Lord Haw Haw was dedicated 'news junkie'

Pat Sidley and news reporters

Meyer "Johnny" Johnson, who has died aged 79, did not have to make *The Citizen* profitable — it was bankrolled by the then National Party government to carry out its mission to propagate the apartheid policies of the NP and smash the liberal *Rand Daily Mail* in the process.

The Citizen, set up in 1976, was a product of the Information Scandal in which the government sought to buy the *Rand Daily Mail* in an effort to counter the English press's liberal views. Eventually, along with other expenditure in local and international propaganda, the information department started *The Citizen.*

The task of becoming profitable, the bugbear of all daily newspapers in this country, could never have been part of his conditions of employment, as the paper under him never made any money. *The Citizen*'s first editor, Martin Spring, had lasted only a matter of weeks.

Johnson carried out his task of being a government mouthpiece with great zeal and R32-million of taxpayers' money. Down the road in Johannesburg, the *Rand Daily Mail*'s owners had fired Raymond Louw as editor of the paper, fearful of the threat *The Citizen* posed, making Johnson's task that much easier. Part of the Information scandal disclosures (eventually published by the *Rand Daily Mail* and *Sunday Express*) showed that many of the government-supporting organisations quoted as sources in his newspaper, were sponsored by the government.

Johnson was never distinguished by any obvious sense of enlightenment. He was rightwing, supported the *verkrampte* end of the now defunct United Party, and supported the NP eventually when very few Jews of Johnson's generation (the Holocaust generation) would have supported it. The party had supported the Germans and had not allowed Jews to join it for many years.

His tenure at the *Sunday Express* was marked by his inability to see and support the changes coming in the United Party when the "Young Turks" split. He left the newspaper embittered and angry when he was not given the editorship of the *Sunday Times* as he believed he was owed.

His role as an employer was marked by eccentricities now legendary. The stories told include vulgar behaviour, forcing reporters to eat their words (literally) and behaviour that would generally be frowned upon these days.

But he had been a president of the journalists' union, The Southern African Society of Journalists (SASJ) and felt an affinity for it over the years. His employers in the Afrikaans press did not allow journalists to belong to the SASJ and that was a policy he followed. But after each annual wage agreement between the English press and the SASJ he would call the SASJ office to find out the details of the agreement so that he could keep vaguely in line with it. Despite his eccentric employment practices, there are many journalists who got their start under his tutelage and were employed by him when other employers declined. Despite his political views, this included several black journalists.

Johnson, who was editor of the *Sunday Express* from 1961 to 1974 and editor of *The Citizen* from 1976 to 1998, began his relationship with the press at the age of 14, when he began working to help support his family. He attended night classes to matriculate. He began work as a copy runner in 1938 at the *Daily Express* and went on to work as a reporter and sub-editor at a number of publications. He worked at the *Sunday Express,* the *Rand Daily Mail, The Star* and the *Sunday Times* before becoming editor of the *Sunday Express.*

Johnson was an idiosyncratic figure, known for his complete dedication to his work and his acerbic temper. But he was also considered a kind and loyal man by those who knew him closely. "He was a very kind man but could be a real maniac when he was angry," says friend and former colleague Patrick Weech. He became renowned for his ability to perform any of the numerous tasks in the print industry. "He was an incredible news editor. He did everything," says Weech.

Johnson, who died in his sleep of cancer, leaves behind his wife, Cecily, three daughters and five grandchildren. He retired in 1998, but, says Weech, he remained a "news junkie" until his death. Nobody would argue that he did not know his craft or understand his readers. But in a South Africa in which inhumanity and injustices abounded, an editor who turned an active blind eye to this was no journalist. He did the job of Lord Haw Haw, and did it better than anyone. **17.01**

LETTERS

Johnson was no Lord Haw Haw

I would like to take issue with the vicious obituary of Johnny Johnson. Lord Haw Haw, real name William Joyce, left Britain for Germany shortly before World War II, after being involved in fascist politics in the United Kingdom. A convinced national socialist, he was appointed editor of Nazi German transmissions to Europe. His wartime broadcasts to Britain became infamous. Captured towards the end of the war, he was charged with treason by a British court, sentenced to death and executed on January 3 1946 in Wandsworth prison.

It is a matter of record that Johnson was no raving leftwinger, no easy man to work with, and edited a government mouthpiece. But he does not deserve to be equated with an arch anti-Semite and Nazi collaborator who was put to death for high treason.
S de Vries, Auckland Park

I wish to congratulate Pat Sidley on an excellent article regarding the passing of MA (Johnny) Johnson, one time editor-in-chief of *The Citizen*. It is with amusement that I recall Johnson's sycophantic "ramblings" in favour of the government of the day, especially during the 1987 elections. Johnson, labelled by some media as "one of South Africa's great editors", had a mediocre editorial career with mediocre tabloids. Hardly the stuff of a Joel Mervis, Lawrence Gandar, Raymond Louw, Jack Patten or John Jordi. — *Robin Parry, Allenby campus, Bramley, 31.01*

How to honour this titan?
Editorial

K*udala u zabalaza, Xhamela!*
After his return from exile, Thabo Mbeki was teaching his mentor and leader, Walter Sisulu, to drive. The novice hiccupped along as learner drivers do, and eventually the mission was aborted. The reason: Sisulu refused to use the hooter to clear children from the streets, insisting instead on stopping the car to shoo them to safety.

Sisulu's humanity is the most important of many virtues to have been highlighted this week, as the nation reflected on his 50 years of political service to South Africa and his unique style of leadership. His life holds lessons for his party, the African National Congress, and for the young nation he helped to shape.

All of us can draw inspiration from a young man who left rural Transkei for Johannesburg in the late 1920s with almost no education, armed with the desire to better himself. He rose from milkman to estate agent at a time when it was rare indeed for black people to own businesses. When, a few years later, the ANC needed his services, Sisulu promptly gave up his new profession to assume the position of secretary general — the movement's first — when there was no guarantee that he would receive a salary.

Unassuming, clear-minded and completely dedicated to the task of developing a mass movement from what had been a "toy telephone" for middle-class leaders, he played a critical role in building the ANC's membership to more than 100 000 by the time it was banned. More than any other factor, it was the growth of the movement among ordinary black South Africans that alarmed the National Party government of Hendrik Verwoerd and triggered the repression of the 1960s that forced the ANC underground.

The Rivonia Trial, where he appeared alongside Nelson Mandela, Govan Mbeki and other leaders after the police raid on Lilliesleaf farm, was perhaps Sisulu's finest hour. It had been decided that to preserve his mythical stature from sniping by formidable state prosecutor Percy Yutar, Mandela would not take the witness stand. Sisulu, as unofficial second-in-command, would assume this role. For three consecutive days he held Yutar at bay, withstanding repeated attempts to draw him into incriminating his fellow accused. It is said that Yutar was so disconcerted that he had him temporarily separated from the other defendants.

To read Sisulu's calm, rational, plain-speaking defence of the ANC's move to armed struggle is a moving experience. Many observers believe that it was his performance in the dock, more than anything else, that saved the Rivonia trialists from the gallows. Never one to sway with intellectual fashion, Sisulu's belief in non-racialism was immovable through 26 years of imprisonment on Robben Island. After the ban on the ANC was lifted in the early 1990s, he would continue his low-profile service to the movement to which he gave his life, routinely appearing for work at its headquarters in Johannesburg. He remained humble and hard-working to the end.

In the new era — when political office frequently comes with power, perks and access to resources — Sisulu's life poses a challenge. His humility, and the fact that he never took government office, are a standing reproach to those in the ruling party whose overmastering concern is to amass power and influence. His ethic of service and self-sacrifice are in marked contrast to those who view the ANC as a passport to the good life. His non-racialism, and openness to diversity and debate, stand in contrast to the lip-service often paid to such democratic values in post-apartheid South Africa. His voice of reason, which often sought to moderate radical posturing and militant rhetoric, his thoughtfulness and plain speaking should serve as an example to present-day populists, particularly in the ANC Youth League, addicted to empty sloganeering.

His life invites party politicians and public servants to revisit their reasons for joining the liberation movement in the first place. His life also invites those of us who are outside political office to become to this nation more than bit players in our own spheres of life. To counter "careerism" and the self-centred politics of faction, the ANC is now calling for the emergence of a "new cadre". The governing party's strategists says this new cadre would be a selfless servant of the nation, who even in the pursuit of individual goals and ambitions would have the interest of fellow citizens at heart. The model for this new cadre already exists. Sisulu, together with others of the ANC old guard, embodied all the values that the new breed should emulate.

And so as he passes on to the next world — a world devoid of prejudice, injustice and inequality — he does so without the earthly honours of office others count as marks of great leadership. But we, the people for whom he lived his life, can reward this titan with the honour he would most appreciate: we must strive to be the human being that he was. **09.05**

LETTER
Sisulu's monument

At St Paul's Cathedral in London there is an inscription paying tribute to its designer Christopher Wren, which in Latin reads: *"Lector, si requiris monumentum circumspice* [Reader, if you require a monument, look around you]." The monument Walter Sisulu left behind was a liberated South Africa wrought through struggle and sacrifice. The enduring quality of this monument will depend on all of us who are left behind. — *Judith February, Cape Town, 23.05*

OFFICE OF THE PRESIDENT

Comrade Walter Sisulu,
c/o The Pearly Gates,
The Entrance to Heaven

URGENT

Dear Walter

I have just received the news of your departure. I immediately sat down to write this letter, confident in the knowledge that, dead or alive, it would reach you. Admittedly, with our postal services, it may take a little while. But I have marked it urgent and I am sure it will get there in the end — which is to say some time before the Last Trumpet is sounded.

And, after all, when one considers that even Robben Island did allow us to send the occasional letter, I have every confidence that the authorities in the parts where you find yourself will want to be seen to be doing a lot better.

I have to tell you there has been a lot of weeping and wailing around here at the news of your going, Walter. You are going to be greatly missed. But then I hardly need to tell you of your popularity. People seemed surprised that I was not joining in the general sobbing and somewhat bewildered when I tried to explain that you had merely gone ahead to do some organising for the African National Congress.

Basically, it appears that people just cannot understand the strength of a friendship like ours. I mean a friendship that can survive your introduction of me to Winnie is not going to have any trouble in coming to terms with death.

I must say I am looking forward to hearing from you, not only to confirm that you are getting on OK (have you started another estate agency?) but in the hope that from your privileged vantage point you will be able to help solve some of the great metaphysical questions of our time.

For instance, when He decided to make man in his own image, does that mean He looks like FW or Thabo?

Why did He unleash PW Botha on the world ? Not to mention Hendrik Verwoerd, JG Strijdom and John Vorster?

Are all 11 languages given official recognition Up There? If not, what is He going to do about it? Does He pay UIF contributions for the angels and are the working hours fair and the levels of pay adequate?

Do they have a written Constitution, a Bill of Rights, a universal franchise and is His reign limited to two terms, like the presidency here? (If not, I guess you and I will have a lot of work to do.)

On the vexed question of Aids and the HI virus, does He think Thabo is as silly as I do?

What did Winnie do with the money?

Do you have any insight, from where you are, as to when Robert Mugabe plans to come out of the cupboard and what he will be wearing for the occasion?

Do They have the pencil test (well, you never know!)?

Where is Tutu?

And so forth and so on.

Old friend, I guess that — as in life — nothing is certain in death and there is a possibility that this letter will never reach you and that I will not be getting a reply. If that is the case then I guess that this is the end of a correspondence that I have greatly enjoyed.

When I look back over that long road to freedom that we trod together, I realise that our story is anyway a never-ending one. It is a story that will not end with the death of you or me, but will be handed on from generation to generation. The story of how two young men, one an estate agent and the other a lawyer, destroyed one nation and replaced it with another much fairer one. A story that, were it not true, would need to be invented, because in so many ways it is so bloody funny.

Hambe kahle, Walter. You can go with pride.

Your friend,

Nelson

LETTER
Best wishes from Walter

Dear Nelson,
I read your letter, in fact I was with you as you wrote it. I'm now light as a feather — if only we could be as light in life. How we burden ourselves with the seriousness of it all — that daily grind. That life we lead ... or is it that life that we live according to what is expected of us?

I'm enjoying this Earth — this gem in a universe. Free, I glide over our beloved continent, the shackles of ownership are gone! What a place! It literally hums with goodwill. A womb with radiant potential. Why expect God to provide us with another paradise when he's provided it already?

If everyone just took a long, hard look in the mirror and promised to be themselves, the real them — that child, that sensitive, creative, happy being, full of wonder — the ripples of laughter would drive away the woes and heal the wounds of the world.

All my laughter,
Walter
(Submitted by Adam Carnegie, Cape Town, 23.05)

Eish, farewell Slow Poison

Fikile-Ntsikelelo Moya

The Orlando Pirates star showered immediately after the match, as he usually did. He jumped into his car and off he went. It was the last time that his fans, friends and teammates would see him alive. That was almost 39 years ago, when Pirates all-time great Eric Bhamuza "Scara" Sono died in a car accident in the Free State. This week Pirates lost Phuthi Lesley Manyathela. For older Pirates supporters and the South African sporting fraternity, that sickening feeling crept back.

Manyathela was said to have been tired after returning from France the previous day. Similar talk of tiredness was bandied about after Sono's accident. He had played in an encounter with Avalon

Athletic at the Indian Sports Ground on Saturday; and kicked off in a friendly against Dobsonville Rangers in Soweto the next day. It would be unfair to compare Sono and Manyathela. For starters "Scara" gave Pirates and South African football its foremost talent in his sons Matsilele Ephraim "Jomo" Sono and the talented yet eccentric Julius "KK" Sono.

To Pirates he was far more than just a player, having being responsible for the recruitment of a spindly Kaizer Motaung and the tricky Percy "Chippa" Moloi. Manyathela may not have recruited anyone to the club, but his contribution to its recent glory is unquestionable. His 18 league goals, the most by any player last season, won the club the championship. In fact it was his goal, coming at the death against Wits University in Phokeng, Rustenburg, that saw the club being crowned South African champions in May. With that goal he had also fulfilled the promise he had made to club boss Irvin Khoza that he would score at least 22 goals (18 in the league and four in cup games) for the season, to match the jersey number he wore.

No great wonder that the club is considering retiring the number. If it does, it would be the second jersey number that the club will stop printing because of a road accident. The first was Clifford "Tough" Moleko's number 13 jersey. "Tough", who was on loan to Cape Town-based Seven Stars at the time, died in 1998.

Although Manyathela's mercurial talents have been praised all round — albeit posthumously — there were times they did not seem obvious to everyone. After setting the amateur scene alight for Shayandima Arsenal in Musina, Limpopo, Manyathela joined then first division team Dynamos on loan. Pirates director of youth development Augusto Palacios spotted him when Palacios was scouring the country looking for suitable players for the under-20 national team he coached at the time. At the same time Kaizer Chiefs scouts had got wind of the youngster's talent. The battle for his signature ensued. Pirates won the day over Chiefs, partly because they offered the youngster's parents more money and — unlike Chiefs, who wanted him to go through their youth team for a season — the club promised him jersey number 22 in the first team.

In July 2000 he made his debut for Pirates in the Vodacom Challenge and created a goal. His detractors could argue that his was a simple tap in, but it was that instinct for being in the right place at the right time, and doing the basics, that would make him stand out among his teenaged peers. But if he thought that that, combined with his tendency to come off the bench and score vital goals, would ensure he would get a regular run in Gordon Igesund's championship-winning team of the 2000/01 season, he was wrong.

It was only with the arrival of Frenchman Jean-Yves Kerjean during the 2001/02 season that Manyathela's immense potential shone through. In that time, scoring seemed to come naturally to him: he was the chief goal-getter for the under-20 and later under-23 teams he featured in.

Manyathela was certainly the lynchpin and the crown jewel in a Pirates teeming with youthful exuberance. Now he is dead. Pirates have lost exceptional players in their prime such as "Asinamali" Metseeme in the mid-1960s and, more recently, Moleko.

But with Slow Poison, *eish* ... **15.08**

'He's an old dog that can't bite'

Brian McDonald

Ugandans are divided about a possible return or burial in home soil for Idi Amin Dada, the former president responsible for a brutal regime under which an estimated 400 000 people were killed or disappeared for ever.

Amin is in critical condition at the King Faisal Specialist Hospital in Jeddah, Saudi Arabia. He has reportedly recently emerged from a week-long coma after suffering from hypertension and kidney complications. He remains in intensive care and doctors are close-lipped about his condition. [Amin died on August 16.]

Speaking at a peace workshop in Kampala this week, President Yoweri Museveni said Amin's family could bring his body back to Uganda, but that he would be buried like any "ordinary Ugandan". Museveni was less sympathetic when asked if the former dictator could return while still alive — as his family has requested. "If Amin comes back breathing or conscious, I will arrest him because he committed crimes here."

Milton Obote, who was deposed by Amin in 1971 and lives in exile in Zambia, has also weighed in, saying in a statement that if Amin died he should be buried in the land of his birth. "Should Amin's condition worsen, the people of Uganda should be magnanimous enough to accept his proper burial in Uganda, despite the fact [that] he was a dictator."

Meanwhile in Kabalagala, a strip of nightclubs, restaurants and open-air bars on Kampala's outskirts, the former dictator's fate was a subject on everyone's lips. "He's an old dog that can't bite and he's on his deathbed, so he can't be of any harm to anyone," Leonard Ssanguuda (29), a driver, said. "The government will be remembered for how they treat their former enemies."

But an administrator, whose life was touched by the dictator's cruel hand, had a very different view. "Like almost everybody else in Uganda, I had a relative who disappeared while Amin was in power and we grew up with that man's children," Sandra Kamenya (28) said. "Unless he's willing to come back and face trial, we don't want him. He's going through the pain people always prayed he would go through and should feel the same agony he caused so many Ugandans."

Chappa Karuhanga, chairperson of the National Democrats Forum Party, was put into a military prison for organising against Amin in 1976. Yet, even though he was supposed to be killed by the man now on his deathbed, the politician isn't calling for vengeance. "We should discuss and debate in Parliament and in public to find a way to bring back these former leaders and deal with them," he said. "But we should be governed by our wish for national reconciliation and nothing else."

Born in 1924 or 1925 into the Kakwa tribe in Arua district, the future "President for Life" had an unprepossessing start. With little formal education, he joined the King's African Rifles of the British colonial army as a private. After seeing action during the brutal Mau Mau revolt in Kenya (1952 to 1956), Amin rose through the ranks to lieutenant.

After independence from Britain in 1962 Obote, the first president, rewarded Amin's loyalty by promoting him to captain in 1963, making him deputy commander of the army in 1964 and finally chief of the army and air force in 1970. Relations with Obote soured and Amin began recruiting members of his own tribe into the army. Then, on hearing that the president was preparing to arrest him for misappropriating army funds, he staged a coup on January 25 1971 while Obote was in Singapore.

Within months of taking control Amin's reign of terror began. He ordered the wholesale massacre of soldiers from tribes he accused of being loyal to Obote while also targeting professionals and intellectuals. Military tribunals took precedence over civil law. Amin filled top government posts with army personnel and anyone thought to be disloyal to the regime was in jeopardy. In 1972 he decided to "Africanise" the economy, and between 50 000 and 70 000 Pakistanis and Indians were given 90 days to leave the country. Their assets were nationalised and later ended up in the hands of the president's cronies. Eventually christening himself "Conqueror of the British Empire" and even "King of Scotland", Amin, a Muslim, strengthened ties with Libya and other Arab nations while alienating the West.

In 1972 he severed diplomatic relations with Israel and in 1976 did the same with Britain. That same year Israeli commandos launched a raid on Entebbe airport to free about 100 passengers on an Air France jet hijacked by Palestinians.

Eventually the country disintegrated into chaos. In one of his final acts Amin invaded Tanzania in late 1978 to cover up an army mutiny. Aided by a group of Ugandan rebels, the Tanzanian army responded, and by April 1979 their combined forces were in Kampala. Amin fled to Libya where he remained for 10 years before finding final asylum in Saudi Arabia. **25.07**

Cardoso's last, greatest report

Paul Fauvet

The Maputo City Court is due to deliver its verdict on January 31 in the case of the six men accused of murdering Mozambique's foremost investigative journalist, Carlos Cardoso, in November 2000.

Carlitos Rashid, the man who fired the shots that ended Cardoso's life, and a second member of the hit squad, Manuel Fernandes, have confessed to their part in the murder. But the man who recruited them, and who drove the car used in the murder, Anibal dos Santos Junior ("Anibalzinho"), was being tried *in absentia*. Someone unlocked his cell door on September 1 and he is now believed to be in South Africa, protected by South African criminals with whom he worked in stolen-car rackets.

Almost five months have passed with no sign of the promised report into the disappearance of Anibalzinho. It is not thought credible that such a high-profile prisoner could be released by bribing a few low-level policemen, and the question repeatedly raised is: did the order to release Anibalzinho come from the Ministry of the Interior?

Anibalzinho's disappearance was very convenient, since he was the link between those who murdered Cardoso and those who ordered the assassination. The prosecution's case against the other three defendants was thus weakened. They are a notorious Maputo loan shark, Momade "Nini" Assife Abdul Satar, his brother Ayob Abdul Satar, who owns the Unicambios Foreign Exchange Bureau, believed to be involved in major money laundering operations, and former bank manager Vicente Ramaya.

Ramaya and members of the Abdul Satar family were key figures in a major fraud, through which the equivalent of R140-million was syphoned out of the the country's largest bank, the Banco Central Moçambique (BCM), on the eve of its privatisation. Cardoso had followed this case tenaciously, demanding that it be brought to trial. When the public and private prosecution lawyers summed up, on January 13, they demanded the maximum penalty for all six accused.

The Cardoso family lawyer, Lucinda Cruz, had no doubt that the main motive for the crime was the BCM fraud. But she did not rule out other motives and other people who may also have ordered the killing. "For the assassination of a person such as Carlos Cardoso, there need not be just one motive," she stressed. Cruz said the crimes could be committed by several people, each with his own motive and "united in a single purpose — to kill someone".

The accusations made in court against others — notably businessman Nyimpine Chissano, the eldest son of President Joaquim Chissano —"deserve to be investigated seriously", said Cruz. Nini Abdul Satar had admitted making payments to Anibalzinho, but claimed he did so at the request of Nyimpine Chissano, and did not realise the money was for a contract killing. Called to the witness stand, Chissano denied all knowledge of Anibalzinho, and said he had only met Abdul Satar once. But one of his associates, rich businesswoman Candida Cossa, testified that she had personally seen Abdul Satar and Chissano together on four occasions.

Even if Chissano had nothing to do with Cardoso's murder, the question remains: Why was a supposedly respectable businessman dealing with such a disreputable character as Abdul Satar? The accusations against Chissano were made late, making it impossible to add him to the list of accused in this trial. Instead, he is the subject of a separate investigation, currently in the hands of the public prosecutor's office. Only this investigation could decide whether Chissano, too, should be brought to trial for the murder. Cruz stressed "it is up to civil society, and the friends of Carlos Cardoso to demand that the investigation continue". They should ensure that the accusations against Chissano and several others "are not forgotten and that this case does not join the heap of other cases that have ground to a halt in the various stages of criminal investigation".

In her impassioned speech, Cruz told the court that this trial, broadcast live on Mozambican radio and TV, "could be regarded as the last and greatest report of Carlos Cardoso. At this trial, a vast number of crimes have been denounced before all of us, including money-laundering, usury, the illegal transfer of foreign exchange, car thefts, bank frauds, trafficking in influence, illegal loans, and corruption in its most varied forms".

The live broadcasts grabbed the attention of all of urban Mozambique. In every city, people could be seen huddled round TV sets or radios listening to the drama. There were even complaints in Maputo that the trial broadcasts were seriously affecting productivity. "The live broadcasts of this trial have achieved what Carlos Cardoso was unable to do while alive," Cruz said. "It has carried his voice to the most remote parts of Mozambique. And it has made us aware that we were losing the moral values that are universally recognised, regardless of political regime or religious creed." Cruz believed there was now enough evidence, thanks to the trial, to open more than 100 new cases, "concerning crimes and illegalities committed by public and private institutions, and by individuals".

Why was Cardoso murdered? Because he was a journalist, Cruz replied — "a journalist who denounced abuses, who did not shut up, who would not forget any matter, who insisted on following what he regarded as most important, and who would not allow any of the illegalities he had written about to fall into oblivion. "Carlos Cardoso was a pain, he was obstinate, he was really inconvenient," she added. "The only way for any criminal to go on practising crimes with impunity was to silence Carlos Cardoso. And the only way to silence Carlos Cardoso was to kill him." **31.01**

All six accused were found guilty. They were sentenced to prison terms of up to 28 years for the murder of Cardoso and the attempted murder of his driver. Anibal dos Santos Jnr was apprehended in South Africa the day before the verdict and was extradited to Mozambique to serve his sentence.

From altar boy to revolutionary

John Matshikiza

It seems to be an unavoidable fact of the human condition that former altar boys, especially the Catholic ones, end up being the best revolutionaries.

Chris Hani grew up in rural Transkei, near Cofimvaba, and got his rudimentary education in Catholic schools, from where it was a natural progression for him, bright lad that he was, to become an altar boy and develop a fierce determination to become a priest when he grew up. Luckily his father put his foot down, vetoing any such plans, and Chris was set on the road to becoming a lifelong revolutionary instead.

Perhaps Catholic priests (and high church Anglicans like Trevor Huddleston) have that much more fervour about their mission — or at least they did in the old days. Perhaps they had a way of putting across the ideas contained in the Christian Bible in a particularly believable way.

Certainly the life of Christ was itself quite a revolutionary one, standing up, as he did, against both Roman colonial occupation and repression, and the reactionary cant of his own religion and society. The guy sure did change the world, although it took some time. And that would have been attractive and significant in the growing mind of the young Chris Hani. But how revolutionary can you get? How determined can you become in the quest to reach that elusive goal of universal liberation?

I can only speculate that it was that early Catholic intensity that turned Chris into the dedicated, single-minded, selfless revolutionary that he was — a selflessness that would ironically also be the cause of his destruction (like Christ's, one might argue, while seeking to avoid straying into the territory of blasphemy).

The more gullible among us would leap at the analogy. "Hey, yeah: 'Chris', 'Christ', 'crucifixion'. There might be something in this!" But that is not in any way where one wants to go. To begin with, the guy we all knew and loved as "Chris" wasn't Chris at all. His real name was Martin Tembisile Hani. He had borrowed his younger brother's name in order to secure a passport from the South African authorities while he was on the run, and used this subterfuge to get out of the country. (Presumably he brushed aside any notion that his kid brother might one day have some use for a passport of his own. The revolutionary impulse is filled with daunting certainties, decisions that have to be taken on the spur of the moment, consequences to be considered at some later time.)

But once out of the country, and through all those revolutionary years, until the day he was killed, he kept his brother's identity — or at least part of it. At no time, not even after coming out from underground and returning to South Africa, did he ever consider reverting to being Martin Hani. Why?

Chris was a funny guy. The former altar boy who was determined to become a priest was an unlikely candidate for a guerrilla. Even in later years it was his intellectual character rather than his physique that impressed you when you met Chris. And yet, in 1963, at the tender age of 21, he, along with a small group of others, had decided that, rather than taking advantage of the ANC leadership's offer to send them abroad for advanced education, priming them for "leadership", he would join the ranks of Umkhonto weSizwe (MK), and become a soldier like any other South African patriot. And he turned out to be the best and most dedicated soldier of that early, post-Rivonia generation — and a natural leader within the ranks of MK.

Those were indescribably difficult times in exile. It was clear that all levels of the ANC and MK were infiltrated. People were advised to choose *noms de guerre* to avoid being identified, and to save their families from persecution back home. I grew up with people who called themselves by unlikely names like Boston Gagarin (also known as Tar Baby), Tau Tau, DB, Sheriff, Champ and so on. Chris kept the name Chris — but, in a half-hearted attempt at concealment, changed his surname to Nkosana. And so we knew him till the 1970s, and everybody's cover was blown anyway, and he reverted — not to his own name, but his brother's. I guess he figured no one, not even his wife, would swallow that "Martin" moniker that he had dropped so long ago. And so "Chris Hani" he stayed.

But at another level, I think that the name he chose to be known by was an indication that he never had any intention of coming out from underground until the final objective had been attained. It had become part of his skin. He had taken a decision, way back in 1963, to throw himself into the struggle for liberation, at whatever cost, and losing his own identity was part of that process. It made no difference to him. What mattered was the final outcome.

I believe that this is what made the man we will always remember as Chris Hani what he was to all of us. Through the long years of exile and underground engagement, Chris was uniquely open, honest, committed, courageous, friendly, loving, humorous, open about his own fallibility and loyal far beyond the call of duty.

Something of all of this shone through Chris, so that even those who did not know him intimately instantly trusted his integrity. To those who had lived through the long, bitter years of struggle, inside and outside the country, Chris Hani was a rare symbol of all the things that were held dear in the concept of commitment and leadership.

Why is his loss so painful even now, 10 years after he was cut down? A friend of mine who marched with Chris all through those years, from 1963 to 1993, says that his loss is important because "Chris, today, would have been the conscience of the African National Congress. No one would have been able to ignore his views. He was not the kind of person who would be tempted to stream into the comfort zones of the new South Africa. He would never have given up the fight for the ordinary people."

For myself, I agree with all of the above. But more than that, I miss him because he was just Chris. **11.04**

> "If we didn't go up in flames then, I don't think we'll ever go up in flames at any other time."
> — Archbishop Desmond Tutu, recalling the volatile situation in South Africa after Chris Hani's death 10 years ago. 11.04